JOSEPH & MARKETPLACE MINISTRY

A SIMPLE GUIDE TO KINGDOM LEADERSHIP

DARRELL "COACH D" ANDREWS
& DR. SHANNON A. AUSTIN

CROWN & QUILL PRESS

"The original purpose for man's creation was not to go to heaven but to dominate the earth. That's what makes marketplace ministry essential—it's about manifesting the Kingdom here and now."
— *Dr. Myles Munroe*
Kingdom Leadership Teacher, Author, and Founder of Bahamas Faith Ministries

"Dream great dreams for God, because when you dream, you give God something to work with."
— *Dr. David Yonggi Cho*
Founding Pastor, Yoido Full Gospel Church, South Korea

"Then God blessed them, and God said to them, 'Be fruitful and multiply; fill the earth and subdue it; have dominion over the fish of the sea, over the birds of the air, and over every living thing that moves on the earth.'"
— *Genesis 1:28 (NKJV)*

Copyright © 2025 by Darrell Andrews and Dr. Shannon A. Austin
All rights reserved.

Published by Darrell Andrews and Dr. Shannon A. Austin / Crown & Quill Press LLC

Paperback ISBN: 978-1-967124-37-4
Hardcover Book ISBN: 978-1-967124-36-7
eBook ISBN: 978-1-967124-39-8
Large Print Edition ISBN: 978-1-967124-38-1

Crown & Quill Press, LLC
United States

No part of this publication may be reproduced, stored in a retrieval system, or transmitted in any form or by any means—electronic, mechanical, photocopying, recording, or otherwise—without the prior written permission of the publisher, except for brief quotations used in reviews, articles, or scholarly works.

Scripture References

Scripture quotations are taken from the following Bible translations:

- *King James Version (KJV)*. Public domain.

- *New King James Version® (NKJV)*. Copyright © 1982 by Thomas Nelson. Used by permission. All rights reserved.

- *English Standard Version (ESV)*. Copyright © 2001 by Crossway, a publishing ministry of Good News Publishers. Used by permission. All rights reserved.

- *New Living Translation (NLT)*. Copyright © 1996, 2004, 2015 by Tyndale House Foundation. Used by permission of Tyndale House Publishers, Carol Stream, Illinois 60188. All rights reserved.

- *Amplified® Bible (AMP)*. Copyright © 1954, 1958, 1962, 1964, 1965, 1987 by The Lockman Foundation. Used by permission. All rights reserved.

- *The Message (MSG)*. Copyright © 1993, 1994, 1995, 1996, 2000, 2001, 2002 by Eugene H. Peterson. Used by permission of NavPress. All rights reserved. Represented by Tyndale House Publishers.

These resources are utilized to enhance biblical understanding and provide deeper theological insight into the original languages of Scripture.

DEDICATION

This book is dedicated to every modern-day Joseph—the dreamers, the builders, and the faithful ones in hidden places.

To the leader who's been overlooked,
To the visionary who's been misunderstood,
To the servant who's stayed faithful in silence,
To the believer who still carries the dream God gave them.

This is for you.

May you never doubt the purpose in your process.
May you trust God's timing, even when the wait is long.
And may you rise to lead with courage, compassion, and Kingdom purpose
as you step into the place He's prepared for you.

We also dedicate this book to our families—
your love, patience, and prayers helped carry us through every season.
To our friends and mentors—thank you for believing in us,
encouraging us when we were tired and reminding us to keep going.
Your words, your support, and your wisdom shaped this message.

To every person who has spoken life into our journey—
you are part of this mantle.
You helped birth something that will bless others for generations to come.

To God be the glory.
May this book go where He sends it and touch the lives He's called it to reach.

— Darrell "Coach D" Andrews & Dr. Shannon A. Austin

CONTENTS

Preface	IX
Introduction	XI
1. Part 1	1
2. Chapter 1	3
3. Chapter 2	10
4. Chapter 3	17
5. Chapter 4	24
6. Chapter 5	31
7. Part 2	37
8. Chapter 6	38
9. Chapter 7	44
10. Chapter 8	50
11. Chapter 9	56
12. Chapter 10	62
13. Part 3	68
14. Chapter 11	69

15.	Chapter 12	79
16.	Chapter 13	85
17.	Chapter 14	94
18.	Chapter 15	100
19.	Acknowledgements	105
20.	About the Authors	107

PREFACE

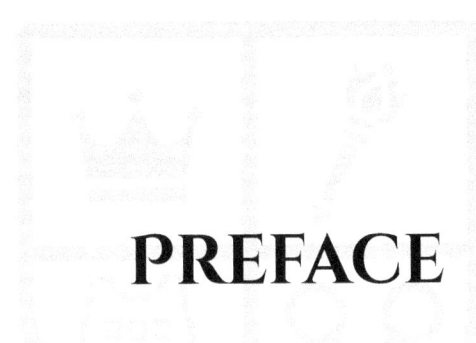

This book was born out of prayer, pain, and purpose. It didn't come from theory—it came from real life. Like many of you, we've walked through seasons that didn't make sense. We've been misunderstood, overlooked, and stretched beyond what we thought we could handle. But in all of it, God was preparing something greater.

We've served in both ministry and the marketplace. We've felt the weight of leadership and the fire of waiting. We've faced closed doors, tight deadlines, and big dreams with few resources. Yet through it all, we've seen God's hand. We've learned that when God gives you a vision, He also gives you the strength to carry it—even when it takes longer than you expected.

This book is for those who know they're called to lead, even if they haven't been given a title. It's for the visionary who's been in a hidden place. It's for the entrepreneur, the educator, the pastor, the professional, and the student. It's for anyone who wants to lead with purpose, faith, and wisdom in the real world.

We believe that God is raising up modern-day Josephs—men and women who carry His heart and His strategy into the world's most important places. These Josephs don't just want to fit in—they're called to stand out. They are leaders with dreams, discernment, and the courage to bring change where it's needed most.

Joseph's life was full of ups and downs. He was betrayed, falsely accused, and forgotten. But he stayed faithful. And in time, God raised him up—not just for himself, but for a whole generation. Joseph didn't just survive—he led. He didn't just lead—he transformed a nation.

That same calling is on you.

You were made to lead with integrity, wisdom, and compassion. You were created to carry solutions and shape culture. You are not here by accident—you were born for impact.

This book will walk you through Joseph's story and connect it to your own. We'll explore what it means to carry the Fourfold Mantle of Joseph—kingship, rulership, priesthood, and ambassadorship. We'll also teach you the Five Kingdom Leadership Principles that unlock purpose, influence, and lasting change.

As you read, pray, and reflect, we believe God will stir something deep inside you. He's preparing you for more. He's calling you to rise.

So get ready.
You're not just reading a book—you're stepping into your assignment.
You are a Joseph.
And your time is now.

INTRODUCTION
A Generation on the Rise

There is a generation rising—leaders, dreamers, and change-makers—who feel a pull toward something greater. You may not have a title, a platform, or public recognition, but deep down, you know you were made for more. Like Joseph, you've held onto a dream through tough seasons. You've stayed faithful through silence, trusted God through the unknown, and kept going even when others didn't understand.

This book is for you.

It's a call to wake up the purpose inside you and boldly step into the assignment God has placed on your life.

> *"Then God blessed them, and God said to them, 'Be fruitful and multiply; fill the earth and subdue it; have dominion over the fish of the sea, over the birds of the air, and over every living thing that moves on the earth.'"* — Genesis 1:28 (NKJV)

From the beginning, God gave us a clear mission: to grow, create, and lead. He called us to rule—not with pride or control, but with purpose, love, and responsibility. This wasn't just a blessing; it was a leadership plan.

God wants us to represent Him in the world by caring for what He created, helping others, and living with integrity.

That same call still exists today. God is raising up leaders in every area of life—people who follow Him and make a difference. You might lead in a business, a school, a church, a home, or a government role. Wherever you are, you are called to bring change.

There are many great books about Joseph, leadership, and the Kingdom of God. But this book brings those ideas together in a new way. It's about how Kingdom leadership works—how it grows in us, how it works through us, and how it changes the world around us.

Joseph's story isn't just a Bible story—it's a leadership guide. He was rejected by family, treated unfairly, and forgotten. But he stayed faithful, and God used him to save lives. Joseph didn't rise to power to fit in—he rose to make a difference. His purpose wasn't just personal. It was for his generation—and ours.

As authors, Darrell "Coach D" Andrews and Dr. Shannon Austin, we've both walked through seasons of pain, pressure, and promotion—just like Joseph. We've led in ministry and in the marketplace. We've seen delays, but we've also seen God's perfect timing. This book comes not just from study but from experience.

We'll walk with you through the Fourfold Mantle of Joseph: kingship, rulership, priesthood, and ambassadorship—four roles that help us walk in purpose. We'll also introduce Five Kingdom Leadership Principles: Visionary Leadership, Crisis Management, Wealth Stewardship, Strategic Influence, and Kingdom Mindset. These are tools that will help you lead with both spiritual depth and everyday wisdom.

Whether you're working in business, education, ministry, media, or government, know this:
You weren't made to just survive the system. You were born to transform it. You carry God's answers for real problems in the world.

You are a modern-day Joseph.
And your time is now.

How to Use This Book

This book is meant to do more than just inspire you—it's here to activate you. It's a leadership manual for modern-day Josephs. It's designed to help you understand your purpose, hear God's voice more clearly, and take action in your calling.

Each chapter will walk you through stories from Joseph's life and connect them to your own. You'll learn how to grow as a leader and walk in your Kingdom purpose.

At the end of every chapter, you'll find five key parts:

- **Reflection Questions**—Simple but deep questions that help you think about your character, calling, and next steps.

- **Faith Steps**—Practical things you can do this week to apply what you've learned.

- **Scripture Meditation**—A powerful Bible verse to keep your heart focused and your spirit encouraged.

- **Meditation Reflection**—A short devotional that helps bring the scripture to life in your leadership journey.

- **A Prayer**—A heartfelt prayer that helps you respond to what God is doing in you and ask for His help as you grow.

You don't have to rush. Pause with each section. Take time to think, write, pray, and listen. Let God speak to you through every word. This is not just a book—it's part of your journey. Whether you lead in a boardroom, a classroom, a ministry, or a home, God wants to shape your heart and strengthen your leadership.

Let this be more than reading.

Let it be your invitation to rise.

Step into the mantle of Joseph.

Lead with purpose, power, and a true Kingdom mindset.

PART I

DISCOVERING YOUR PURPOSE IN THE MARKETPLACE

Focus: Learning how to find your vision, calling, and purpose for leadership and business.

CHAPTER 1
A DREAM BIGGER THAN YOU

"Now Israel loved Joseph more than all his children, because he was the son of his old age. Also he made him a tunic of many colors." —Genesis 37:3 (NKJV)

Joseph was only a teenager when God gave him a special dream. One night, he saw bundles of wheat in a field. His bundle stood up straight, and the bundles of his brothers bowed down to it. In another dream, the sun, moon, and eleven stars all bowed to him.

Joseph didn't fully understand what these dreams meant, but he felt in his heart that they came from God. He was excited and shared them with his brothers and father. He thought they would be amazed at what God was showing him. But their reaction was the opposite.

"There we were, binding sheaves in the field. Then behold, my sheaf arose and also stood upright; and indeed your sheaves stood all around and bowed down to my sheaf... Then he dreamed still

> *another dream and told it to his brothers... 'the sun, the moon, and the eleven stars bowed down to me.'"* — Genesis 37:7, 9 (NKJV)

His brothers became jealous and angry. "Do you really think you'll rule over us?" they asked. Even his father didn't understand and corrected him. Joseph felt hurt and confused.

> *"And his brothers said to him, 'Shall you indeed reign over us? ... So they hated him even more for his dreams and his his word... but his father kept the matter in mind."* — Genesis 37:8, 11 (NKJV)

Joseph had shared something that felt important, but he was met with rejection. Even though he didn't see it yet, God had given him a vision of the future. One day, Joseph would become a leader in Egypt and help save many lives. The dream wasn't about pride—it was about purpose.

Dreams Take Time

When God gives a dream, it doesn't usually happen right away. Joseph didn't go from dreaming to leading overnight. Many years passed between the dream and its fulfillment. And those years were filled with hard challenges.

Joseph was sold by his brothers, falsely accused, and thrown into prison. People who promised to help him forgot about him. But even in those painful times, Joseph stayed faithful. He trusted God, even when he didn't understand what was happening.

God used that waiting season to grow Joseph's character. Joseph had to learn humility, patience, and leadership. God was preparing him to carry the weight of the dream. The same is true for us.

> *"If any of you lacks widsom, let him ask of God, who gives to all liberally and without reproach."* — James 1:5 (NKJV)

Your Dream Isn't Just for You

At first, Joseph thought his dream was just about him. But over time, he realized it was about helping others. His leadership would save Egypt and nearby nations—including his own family. His dream had a much bigger purpose.

God gives us dreams not just to bless us, but to bless others through us. Maybe your dream is to build something, lead something, or serve others in a special way. If it's from God, it will always be bigger than you. It will point people to God.

> *"And whatever you do, do it heartily, as to the Lord and not to men... for you serve the Lord Christ."* —Colossians 3:23-24 (NKJV)

Even when people don't support your calling, don't give up. God will give you the strength to carry it out. Keep going, even when it's hard. Joseph didn't give up—and in time, his dream became real.

You Are the Church—Everywhere You Go

Joseph didn't live out his calling in a temple. He served in a prison, in a palace, and in a foreign land. Still, God was with him everywhere. That shows us that God doesn't just work inside church buildings.

As believers, we are the Church. That means we carry God's presence with us wherever we go—school, work, stores, or job sites. The Bible calls us "living stones" that God is building into a spiritual house.

> *You also, as living stones, are being built up a spiritual house...to offer up spiritual sacrifaces acceptable to God through Jesus Christ."* — 1 Peter 2:5 (NKJV)

The Church isn't a place—it's the people of God. We don't leave the Church after Sunday service—we bring it with us into the world. Every space you enter is a place where God can shine through you.

> *"And He put all things under His feet, and gave Him to be head over all things to the church, which is His body"* — Ephesians 1:22-23 (NKJV)

Living as a Kingdom Citizen

Joseph lived in Egypt, but he never forgot who he belonged to. He stayed faithful to the God of Israel. He didn't follow Egypt's false gods. He led with wisdom and integrity, even in a foreign land.

That's what it means to live as a Kingdom citizen. You belong to God's Kingdom first, no matter where you work or live. You carry His values, His love, and His truth. You represent Heaven on Earth.

> *"Now, therefore, you are no longer strangers and foreigners, but fellow citizens with the saints and members of the household of God."* —Ephesians 2:19 (NKJV)

Paul said we are "ambassadors for Christ." An ambassador represents their home country in another place. That's what you are in the world. You represent Jesus in your job, school, and community.

> *"Now then, we are amabassadors for Christ."* — 2 Corinthians 5:20 (NKJV)

The Marketplace Is a Mission Field

Jesus said, "The harvest is plentiful, but the workers are few." This means many people are searching for hope and truth. You may be the only Bible some people ever see. Your life and actions can speak for God.

> *"The harvest truly is plentiful, but the laborer are few."* — Matthew 9:37 (NKJV)

Marketplace ministry isn't about preaching to everyone. It's about showing God's love in how you work, speak, and serve. When you work with honesty and kindness, people notice. Your light will shine.

> *"Let your light so shine before men, that they may see your good works and glorify your Father in heaven."* — Matthew 5:16 (NKJV)

Joseph led with wisdom and saved lives. You can lead with faith and change lives too. You don't need a big title—just be faithful where you are. That's how Kingdom influence begins.

Reflection Questions

1. What leadership quality from Joseph's life do you need to grow in most?

2. How can you show more honesty, wisdom, or humility in your daily work or service?

3. Are there areas where your goals or choices need to better match God's ways?

Faith Steps

- Pick one trait from Joseph's life—like faithfulness or honesty—and practice it this week.

- Think about your personal or work goals. Write down three ways to line them up with God's purpose.

- Pray for wisdom in your decisions and ask God to guide your leadership.

Scripture Meditation

"The Lord was with Joseph, and he [even though a slave] became a successful and prosperous man; and he ws in the house of his master, the Egyptian. NOw his master saw that the Lord was with him and that the Lordcaused all that he did to prosper (succeed) in his hand. So Joseph pleased Potiphar and found favor in his sight, and he served him; and his maser made him supervisor over his house, and he put all that eh owned in Joseph's charge."
— Genesis 39:2-4 (AMP)

Meditation Reflection

Joseph didn't become successful just by working hard—he succeeded because God was with him. Even while he was a slave, God helped him do well. This shows us that when God is with us, we can succeed even in hard places.

Key Meditation Points

- **God's Favor Leads to Success:** Joseph grew in influence because he stayed close to God.

- **Growth in Tough Places:** Joseph didn't let his situation stop him. We can grow, too, even when life feels hard.

- **Faithfulness Matters:** Joseph's character opened doors. God honors faithfulness.

Prayer for Leadership and Guidance

Dear God,
Thank you for the example of Joseph. Help me stay faithful and do what's right, even when life is tough. Lead me in every choice I make, and teach me to trust You more. I want to lead with kindness, strength, and purpose. Please guide my steps and use me to make a difference. In Jesus' Name, Amen.

CHAPTER 2
Trusting the Vision

"Write the vision and make it plain on tablets, that he may run who reads it. For the vision is yet for an appointed time... though it tarries, wait for it because it will surely come." —Habakkuk 2:2-3 (NKJV)

When God gives someone a vision or dream, it doesn't always come with full instructions. Sometimes, it starts with a gentle tug in your heart, a powerful dream in the night, or a moment during prayer when something just "clicks." These moments often feel personal and meaningful, but they may also be confusing or unclear. That's how it was for Joseph. He didn't ask for a dream—God gave it to him, and that dream became the starting point of his journey.

Joseph saw something powerful in his dream: one day, he would be in a place of great leadership and influence. But instead of stepping right into success, Joseph's life became harder. His brothers turned against him and sold him into slavery. Later, he was falsely accused and thrown into prison. It seemed like everything was going wrong—but Joseph never gave up on what God had shown him.

That's what it means to trust the vision. God often gives us a glimpse of the future long before it happens. Sometimes, that vision is meant to stretch us, to prepare us for what's coming. It's not always about where we are right now—it's about where God is leading us. And getting there takes time, faith, and growth.

Kingdom Vision: Seeing from God's Point of View

There's a big difference between a personal dream and a Kingdom vision. A personal dream might focus on your own success, comfort, or achievements. But a Kingdom vision is about what God wants to do through your life to help others and show His love. It's like getting a peek at Heaven's blueprint for your life. Proverbs 29:18 says, *"Where there is no vision, the people perish"* (KJV), which reminds us how important it is to see life from God's perspective.

Joseph's dream wasn't just about being important—it was about saving lives. Many years after his dream, Joseph became a leader in Egypt during a terrible famine. Because of his wisdom, he was able to provide food to people across the land, including the very family that once betrayed him. His vision had purpose far beyond his own life. That's what makes a Kingdom vision so powerful—it blesses others, not just ourselves.

God still plants these kinds of visions in people's hearts today. You might feel a pull to start a business, build a school, or speak up for those without a voice. These ideas may seem small or scary, but when God is behind them, they can grow into something life-changing. A Kingdom vision invites us to partner with God and bring His goodness into the world.

God Calls You Before You're Ready

When God gives you a dream, He usually gives it before you're fully ready to live it out. That's because part of the journey is preparation. Joseph was just 17 when he had his dream, but he wasn't ready to rule a nation. Still, God knew what Joseph would become. Jeremiah 1:5 says, *"Before I formed you in the womb, I knew you."* That means God knew your purpose before you were even born.

You might feel like you don't have what it takes. Maybe you feel too young, too ordinary, or too broken to be used by God. But God doesn't wait for perfection—He walks with you through the process. Every job, mistake, victory, and challenge shapes you. Each step builds the strength and wisdom you'll need to carry out the vision He's placed in your heart.

God's plans often start in hidden places. They begin in quiet moments of prayer, in your journal, or even in your pain. The same way Joseph learned through loss, hard work, and faithfulness, we grow through what we go through. God's preparation is just as important as the vision itself. Trust that He is building you behind the scenes.

Write It Down and Wait for It

One of the most important things you can do when God gives you a vision is write it down. Habakkuk 2:2–3 says, *"Write the vision and make it plain... For the vision is yet for an appointed time... Though it tarries, wait for it; because it will surely come."* Writing down your vision helps you remember what God said, especially when things get tough. It becomes a reminder when you feel lost or discouraged.

After writing your vision, be prepared to wait. God doesn't always move on our timeline. He gives the vision early so that we'll grow, mature, and build the character needed to carry it out. Waiting doesn't mean God has forgotten—it means He is getting everything in place. The dream is still alive, even when it seems delayed.

Sometimes the waiting is where the most growth happens. It's where we learn patience, trust, and humility. Joseph waited for years, but every delay was part of God's perfect plan. Don't rush the process. Trust that God is working all things together in His perfect timing.

Don't Be Afraid of Delays

Delays can feel discouraging, but they are often part of God's design. Joseph did everything right in Potiphar's house, yet he was still accused and imprisoned. Even when he helped others, he was forgotten. But none of those setbacks stopped God's plan—they were part of Joseph's training for leadership. Isaiah 55:8–9 reminds us, *"For My thoughts are not your thoughts, nor are your ways My ways," says the Lord.*

When things aren't happening the way you hoped, it's easy to feel like God has forgotten about you. But He hasn't. Sometimes He delays your breakthrough to protect you or to strengthen you. Other times, He's preparing the right people or opportunities that you don't even know about yet.

Delays are not the end of your story—they are the shaping of it. God sees more than we can, and He knows the best time for your vision to come to life. Stay faithful in the in-between moments. That's where your character grows strong and your faith is made real.

Overcoming Fear, Doubt, and Discouragement

When you step into something new, fear will try to hold you back. You may wonder, "Am I really good enough for this?" Joseph had many chances to give up—after all, he was rejected, enslaved, and thrown into prison. But through it all, he kept trusting God. He believed that the same God who gave him the dream would also bring it to pass.

Sometimes people will doubt your vision, or even try to stop you. That can hurt, especially when it comes from people you care about. But your dream doesn't need their permission—it needs your obedience to God. Joshua 1:9 says, *"Be strong and of good courage... for the Lord your God is with you wherever you go."*

Even when things look like they're falling apart, God is holding the pieces together. Joseph's biggest breakthrough came after his lowest moment. In one day, he went from prison to the palace. God can move that quickly. All He needs is your faith and willingness to keep going.

Romans 8:28 gives us a powerful promise: *"And we know that all things work together for good to those who love God, to those who are the called according to His purpose."* That means even your mistakes, delays, and disappointments can become part of the plan. God is always working behind the scenes.

Stay Focused and Keep God First

As the dream starts to unfold, don't forget the One who gave it to you. It's easy to chase the vision and lose sight of God. But true success comes from walking closely with Him. Matthew 6:33 reminds us, *"Seek first the kingdom of God and His righteousness, and all these things shall be added to you."*

Make prayer a regular part of your routine. Ask God for guidance in your decisions and strength in your challenges. Proverbs 3:5–6 says, *"Trust in the Lord with all your heart... and He shall direct your paths."* That promise is for you—He will show you where to go.

Joseph didn't just achieve success—he honored God while doing it. He led with humility, forgave his brothers, and served with wisdom. That's what real leadership looks like. If you stay faithful, focused, and full of faith, God will finish what He started in your life.

Your vision will come to life—and it will bless more people than you ever imagined.

Reflection Questions

1. What dream or goal has God placed in your heart for leadership, business, or making a difference?

2. How can you rewrite your personal mission in a way that clearly reflects God's purpose?

3. What can you do this week to keep Jesus at the center of what you're called to do?

Faith Steps

- **Take Time to Reflect:** Set aside 30 minutes this week to pray and think about the vision you believe God gave you. Ask Him for clarity and direction.

- **Write Down Your Vision:** Be specific about what you feel called to do. What problems are you drawn to solve? What kind of impact do you hope to make?

- **Choose One Action Step:** Pick one thing you can do this week to move closer to that vision. Maybe it's reaching out to a mentor, joining a group, or volunteering somewhere meaningful.

- **Take the First Step:** No step is too small. God blesses movement and obedience.

Scripture Meditation

For I know the thoughts that I think toward you, says the Lord, thoughts of peace an not of evil, to give you a future and a hope." — Jeremiah 29:11 (NKJV)

Meditation Reflection

God's plans for you are full of peace and hope. Even if things feel uncertain or delayed, God is still leading you. Joseph had big dreams, but he had to wait many years to see them come true. During that time, he faced betrayal, prison, and challenges.

Just like Joseph, you may be in a waiting season. But that doesn't mean your dream is over. God uses those quiet times to shape your heart, build your strength, and prepare you for what's ahead. Waiting is part of the journey—and part of your growth.

Key Meditation Points

- **Vision Takes Time:** Joseph's dreams didn't happen right away. God showed him the end, but the journey came with twists and turns that prepared him.

- **Challenges Are Part of the Plan:** Hard times didn't stop God's purpose for Joseph. The same is true for you—your setbacks can shape your success.

- **Faithfulness Builds Trust:** Joseph gave his best wherever he was. How we handle today shows God we're ready for tomorrow.

- **God's Timing is Perfect:** As Habakkuk 2:3 says, even if the vision takes time, it will happen when the time is right.

Prayer for Vision and Trust

Dear God,
Thank You for the vision You've placed in my heart. Help me to trust You when things take longer than I expected. Remind me that every part of my journey has a purpose, even the hard parts. Give me the courage to take steps toward that vision and the patience to wait on Your timing. Help me to keep You at the center of all I do and to lead in a way that brings You glory. In Jesus' name, Amen.

CHAPTER 3
SHAPING CULTURE WITH KINGDOM INFLUENCE

"You are the light of the world. A city that is set on a hill cannot be hidden. Nor do they light a lamp and put it under a basket, but on a lampstand, and it gives light to all who are in the house. Let your light so shine before men, that they may see your good works and glorify your Father in heaven."
—Matthew 5:14–16 (NKJV)

Joseph's story shows us that God doesn't just want us to succeed for ourselves—He wants us to bring His influence into the world. God gave Joseph more than a dream. He gave him a mission. Joseph's leadership helped shape the culture, economy, and government of Egypt during a time of crisis. God used Joseph to save lives and lead with wisdom in a place far from home.

Joseph went from being a prisoner to being second-in-command over all of Egypt. That promotion wasn't just about him—it was about his ability to bring God's principles into Egypt's systems. Through Joseph, God created a plan that saved food, protected people during a famine, and even reunited a broken family. As Genesis 50:24–25 reminds us, Joseph believed God's promises and trusted that his leadership would bless future generations.

God wants to use you the same way. He places His people in schools, businesses, governments, and communities to be a light—to show what love, truth, and wisdom look like in action. Joseph didn't try to make a name for himself. He faithfully served until God opened the right doors.

What Is Kingdom Culture?

Kingdom Culture means living by God's values, no matter where you are. It's not about rules or religion—it's about bringing the atmosphere of Heaven into everyday life. It's marked by love, peace, joy, truth, and justice. This kind of culture isn't built by being loud or forceful—it's built by people who live humbly and serve others.

In the Bible, Jesus showed us Kingdom Culture by serving with kindness and humility. He said in Mark 10:45 that He came not to be served, but to serve and give His life for many. That's our example—serving others in love, even in hard places.

Joseph followed this same example. He didn't seek power for himself—he used it to help others. He led Egypt with wisdom and kindness, storing grain and sharing it fairly during the famine. His actions reflected God's heart for justice, just like Psalm 112:5–6 says, *"A good man deals graciously and lends; he will guide his affairs with discretion. Surely he will never be shaken; the righteous will be in everlasting remembrance."* —*Psalm 112:5–6 (NKJV)*

Leading Like Joseph

Joseph didn't just lead with his head—he led with his heart. He stayed close to God, even when life was unfair. He forgave the people who hurt him. He led with humility, following the example found in *Colossians 3:23–24*: *"And whatever you do, do it heartily, as to the Lord and not to men, knowing that from the Lord you will receive the reward of the inheritance; for you serve the Lord Christ."*

Godly leaders shape the world by staying true to what's right. Joseph didn't cheat or lie to get ahead. He worked hard, made smart choices, and always gave credit to God. Genesis 41:16 shows this when Joseph told Pharaoh, *"It is not in me; God will give Pharaoh an answer of peace."*

In the same way, you can lead in your school, job, or community. You might not be in charge of a country like Joseph, but you can still show integrity, compassion, and faith. That's how culture begins to change—one leader at a time.

Transforming the World Around You

God has a plan for every part of society. He wants to bring His truth into government, education, business, media, family, and more. These are often called the Seven Cultural Pillars of Influence. *Romans 12:18 reminds us, "If it is possible, as much as depends on you, live peaceably with all men."* That means bringing peace and truth wherever you go.

God uses His people to bring light into these areas:

- **Government**: Leading with honesty and justice.
- **Business**: Serving people through fair, honest work.
- **Education**: Teaching truth and shaping young minds.
- **Media**: Sharing messages of hope and truth.
- **Arts & Entertainment**: Creating beauty that reflects God.
- **Family**: Building strong relationships full of love and grace.
- **Ministry**: Helping others know God's heart.

You don't have to be a pastor to serve God. He uses teachers, nurses, musicians, builders, and more. Wherever He places you, that place becomes your mission field.

Joseph and the Pillars of Culture

Joseph influenced many of these cultural areas. He helped Pharaoh govern wisely and prepared Egypt for years of famine. He managed food and money, helped people during crises, and forgave the brothers who betrayed him. His leadership changed a nation.

Joseph didn't do this from a church pulpit. He did it from a palace, using skills and wisdom God gave him. Proverbs 22:29 says, *"Do you see a man who excels in his work? He will stand before kings."* Joseph's excellence opened doors for influence, and yours can too.

Influence Through Grace

One of the biggest lessons from Joseph's life is this: God's grace opens doors—but character keeps them open. Joseph didn't climb to power through tricks or ambition. He stayed faithful through every test and trial.

When he reached the top, Joseph didn't forget who gave him the dream. He gave God credit, stayed humble, and served well. As James 1:5 says, *if we need wisdom, we should ask God—and He will give it freely.*

That's Kingdom influence. It's not loud or proud. It serves. It leads with love. And it lasts because it's built on truth and trust.

You Are Called to Influence

You might be wondering, "Can God really use me?" Yes, He can—and He will. God places His people in all kinds of places to be lights in dark spaces. He doesn't need you to be famous—just faithful.

Romans 8:28 reminds us that God works all things together for good when we love Him and walk in His purpose. Your experiences, skills, and even your struggles can all be used for something greater.

Ask yourself:

- What breaks my heart?
- What gifts do I have that can help someone?
- Who can I serve right now?

You don't need to be perfect—just available. Start small. Stay consistent. And know that God is using you to shape culture, just like Joseph did.

Reflection Questions

1. Which of the Seven Cultural Pillars do you feel God is calling you to impact?

2. How can you show Kingdom values like honesty, generosity, and humility in your current role?

3. What's one step you can take this week to align your leadership with God's plan?

Faith Steps

- **Know Your Calling:** Choose one of the Seven Pillars—Government, Education, Business, Media, Arts & Entertainment, Religion, or Family—that you feel called to influence.

- **Grow Your Character:** Focus this week on showing the fruit of the Spirit (Galatians 5:22-23) in your daily actions.

- **Invite God In:** Spend time with God and ask Him to guide your leadership and open the right doors.

- **Take One Step:** Do something practical that reflects Kingdom values—such as helping a co-worker, leading with kindness, or resolving conflict with grace.

Scripture Meditation

"Trust in the Lord with all your heart, and lean not on your own understanding; in all your ways acknowledge Him, and He shall direct your paths." — Proverbs 3:5-6 (NKJV)

Meditation Reflection

God wants His people to lead with purpose in every area of society. Like Joseph, Esther, and Daniel, we're called to bring His light into the world through our work, leadership, and actions. God gives influence not for our own benefit but to show His love and truth to others.

Joseph didn't chase after power. His leadership came from trusting God, doing the right thing, and staying faithful through every season. In the same way, real influence starts with a surrendered heart and a strong character.

When we trust God and walk in humility, He opens the right doors and gives us strength to lead well. True leadership is about serving others, staying faithful, and using our influence for God's glory—not just personal gain.

Key Meditation Points

- **Integrity Is Key:** Leading with honesty and humility builds trust and lasting influence.

- **God's Favor Opens Doors:** Like Joseph, you don't need to force your way forward—God will make a way when you trust Him.

- **Character Builds Influence:** The fruit of the Spirit helps you lead with kindness, patience, and self-control.

- **Small Steps Matter:** Faithfulness in the little things prepares you for greater opportunities.

Prayer for Influence and Grace

Dear God,
Thank You for giving me a chance to lead and make a difference. Help me to lead with a humble heart and strong character. Grow the fruit of the Spirit in me—love, joy, peace, patience, kindness, goodness, faithfulness, gentleness, and self-control. Guide my choices, open the right doors, and let Your favor go before me. Help me to be faithful in both small and big tasks so I can honor You with my leadership. May everything I do reflect Your love and truth. In Jesus' name, Amen.

CHAPTER 4

REFINED IN THE FIRE — HOW GOD SHAPES A LEADER'S HEART

> *"Now when they saw him afar off, even before he came near them, they conspired against him to kill him. Then they said to one another, 'Look, this dreamer is coming! Come therefore, let us now kill him and cast him into some pit; and we shall say, "Some wild beast has devoured him." We shall see what will become of his dreams!'" —Genesis 37:18–20 (NKJV)*

Every great leader faces hard times. Whether it's betrayal, failure, or feeling stuck, God often uses these moments to prepare people for something greater. Joseph's story shows us how God can take the worst seasons of our lives and use them to build strong, trustworthy leaders. God didn't raise Joseph to power overnight. First, He shaped Joseph's heart, teaching him to trust, forgive, and grow through the pain.

In God's Kingdom, true leadership isn't about fame, money, or power. It's about having a strong character—someone who chooses honesty, love, and faith, even when no one is watching. Joseph became that kind of person during his trials. The time he spent in slavery and prison wasn't wasted. It was where God taught him wisdom, humility, and perseverance.

What is Kingdom Character?

Kingdom Character is when our actions, thoughts, and decisions reflect Jesus. It's not about being perfect—but about letting God change us from the inside out. God wants His leaders to be kind, honest, patient, and strong, especially during tough times.

This kind of character doesn't just come naturally. It's shaped in hard moments—when someone betrays us, when we lose something, or when we feel alone. God uses those times to teach us to lean on Him and become more like Jesus.

What is Kingdom Ethics?

Kingdom Ethics are the values that guide how we live and treat others. Instead of just doing what seems right to us or following what's popular, we live by God's truth. That means choosing to forgive, speak the truth in love, and treat others fairly—even when it's hard.

Joseph chose these Kingdom ethics when he was tempted, falsely accused, and left in prison. He stayed faithful, didn't lie or seek revenge, and honored God every step of the way. Colossians 3:13 (NJKV) urges us to walk in grace, *"bearing with one another, and forgiving one another, if anyone has a complaint against another; even as Christ forgave you, so you also must do."*

What is a Kingdom Mindset?

A Kingdom Mindset means we look at life the way God does. Instead of focusing on fear or failure, we see every season—good or bad—as part of God's bigger plan. *"Let this mind be in you which was also in Christ Jesus." (Philippians 2:5, NKJV)*

We ask, "What is God teaching me right now?" instead of "Why is this happening to me?" Joseph had this mindset. Even in prison, he believed God had not forgotten him. He kept doing his best, helping others, and staying ready for whatever God had next.

Joseph's Trials—A Setup for His Destiny

Joseph's story takes a hard turn when his brothers turn against him. They were jealous of his dreams and his father's love. One day, they threw him into a pit and sold him as a slave. Genesis 37:19–22 recounts the plot against Joseph:

> *"Then they said to one another, 'Look, this dreamer is coming! Come therefore, let us now kill him and cast him into some pit; and we shall say, "Some wild beast has devoured him." We shall see what will become of him dreams!' But Reuben heard it, and he delivered him out of their hands, and said, 'Let us not kill him.' And Reuben said to them, 'Shed no blood, but cast him into this pit which is in the wilderness, and do not lay a hand on him'-*

That was Joseph's first big test. He was young, scared, and betrayed by his own family. But God didn't leave him. Even in slavery, God gave him favor.

Joseph worked in Potiphar's house and did everything with excellence. But then Potiphar's wife lied about him, and Joseph was thrown into prison.

> *"But the Lord ws with Joseph and showed him mercy, and He gave him favor in the sight of the keeper of the prison."* — Genesis 39:21 (NKJV

In prison, Joseph could have given up. But instead, he kept trusting God. He helped others and grew in wisdom. These painful seasons—betrayal, slavery, and prison—were actually preparing him for leadership in Egypt.

God Uses Trials to Prepare Leaders

Sometimes we think trials are a sign that God is far away. But in Joseph's life—and in ours—trials often mean God is close and working on something big. These difficult seasons make us stronger. They teach us to depend on God, not on our own strength.

> "My brethren, cout it all joy when you fall into various trials, knowing that the testing of your faith produces patience." — James 1:2-3 (NKJV)

Like Joseph, we learn to be patient and stay faithful. Even when we don't understand everything, we can trust that God is getting us ready for more. *"Set your mind on things above, not on things on the earth." (Colossians 3:2, NKJV)* A Kingdom mindset lifts our eyes to God's bigger purpose.

The Power of Forgiveness in Leadership

Joseph could have stayed angry at his brothers or at Potiphar's wife. But he chose something better: forgiveness.

> "But as for you, you meant evil against me; but God meant it for good, in order to bring it about as it is this day, to save many people alive." — Gensis 50:20 (NKJV)

Forgiveness helps leaders stay free. When we let go of hurt and trust God to bring justice, we remain healthy and strong on the inside. Forgiveness doesn't excuse the wrong—it simply says, "God, I trust You to handle it."

"Beloved, do not avenge yourselves, but rather give place to wrath; for it is written, 'Vengeance is Mine, I will repay,' says the Lord." — Romans 12:19 (NKJV)

Jesus also taught us a higher way: *"But I say to you, love your enemies, bless those who curse you, do good to those who hate you, and pray for those who spitefully use you and persecute you."* — Matthew 5:44 (NKJV) That kind of love is powerful—and it changes everything.

What You're Going Through Has Purpose

God used every part of Joseph's life—good and bad—to prepare him for his future. He will do the same with you. Even if your dream feels far away, trust that the hard things are not wasted.

> *"And Pharaoh said to Joseph, 'See, I have set you over all the land of Egypt.'"* — Genesis 41:41 (NKJV)

Joseph's faithfulness led to great influence, and yours will too. But first, let God do the deep work in your heart. *"Be transformed by the renewing of your mind."* (Romans 12:2, NKJV) The fire may feel hot now, but it's shaping you into a leader who shines with God's love and truth.

Reflection Questions

1. What challenge or setback has God used to shape your character?

2. Are there areas in your leadership where you need to stop striving and start trusting God's timing?

3. How can you begin to see your trials as preparation for a

greater purpose?

Faith Steps

- **Reflect on a Challenge:** Think about a recent difficulty and ask God what He is teaching you through it.

- **Write Down a Lesson:** Choose one thing you've learned from a past hardship that could help you now.

- **Choose to Forgive:** Let go of any bitterness or disappointment by forgiving someone who has hurt or failed you.

Scripture Meditation

"In this you greatly rejoice, though now for a little while, if need be, you have been grieved by various trials, tht the genuineness of your faith, being much more precious than gold that perishes, though it is tested by fire, may be found to praise, honor, and glory at the reveloation of Jesus Christ."
— 1 Peter 1:6 – 7 (NKJV)

Meditation Reflection

Tough seasons can feel long, painful, and confusing. But God uses trials to build us. Like Joseph, who went through betrayal, slavery, and prison, we often face challenges before stepping into our calling. These moments aren't wasted—they're shaping us for something greater.
1 Peter 1 reminds us that our faith is more valuable than gold, and it's tested in the fire of life. Just as gold is purified through heat, God uses hard times to develop our strength, character, and trust in Him. Joseph stayed faithful, even when everything seemed unfair, and God used that faithfulness to prepare him for leadership.

Instead of giving in to fear or frustration, we can choose to see these challenges as part of God's process. He's refining us so we can carry greater influence with humility, wisdom, and grace.

Key Meditation Points

- **Trials Prepare You for Purpose:** Difficult seasons are not the end—they're part of the journey that shapes who you're becoming.

- **Faithfulness Builds Strength:** Like Joseph, your response in hard times reveals your readiness for future leadership.

- **Forgiveness Frees Your Heart:** Letting go of offense creates space for healing and keeps your heart open to God's direction.

Prayer for Strength and Refinement

Dear God,
Thank You for being with me in every season—even the hard ones. Help me trust that You are using my challenges to grow me. When I face disappointment or delay, remind me that You are still working behind the scenes. Give me the strength to stay faithful and the courage to forgive. Refine my heart like gold in the fire. Help me become the leader You've called me to be—full of love, wisdom, and grace. In Jesus' name, Amen.

CHAPTER 5

EMBRACING THE HIDDEN SEASON — GROWTH IN OBSCURITY

"Wait on the Lord; be of good courage, and He shall strengthen your heart; Wait, I say, on the Lord!"—Psalm 27:14 (NKJV)

Before Joseph became a leader in Egypt, he spent many years in hard and hidden places. These were not wasted years. God used them to shape Joseph's heart, build his character, and prepare him for something greater. Joseph went through betrayal, slavery, and time in prison. But through it all, God was with him.

Sometimes, God allows us to go through seasons of hiddenness. These are times when we might feel unseen or unrecognized, yet they are not punishment—they are preparation. Just like a seed must be buried in the ground before it can grow, leaders must go through quiet seasons to become strong and fruitful. This hidden period is where true growth happens.

Jesus explained this process clearly: *"Listen carefully: Unless a grain of wheat is buried in the ground, dead to the world, it is never any more than a grain of wheat. But if it is buried, it sprouts and reproduces itself many times over. In the same way, anyone who holds on to life just as it is destroys that life. But if you let it go, reckless in your love, you'll have it forever, real and eternal. If any of you want to serve me, then follow me. Then you'll be where I am, ready to serve at a moment's notice. The Father will honor and reward anyone who serves me."* —John 12:24–26 (MSG)

Joseph's hidden years were like a seed being planted. He served faithfully, even when no one noticed. He never chased attention or fought for promotion. Instead, he trusted God through every hardship. And when the time was right, God raised him up to a position of great influence.

Seasons of Obscurity Help Us Grow

Hidden seasons are important for every leader. They are the times when God works deep inside us. In these seasons, we learn to trust Him, depend on Him, and live with integrity. Joseph's years as a slave and prisoner were hard, yet they prepared him to lead an entire nation.

Even when it felt like no one saw him, God did. *"For God is not unjust to forget your work and labor of love which you have shown toward His name, in that you have ministered to the saints and do minister."* —Hebrews 6:10, NKJV)

Joseph in Prison—Remaining Faithful

Even when Joseph was wrongly accused and thrown into prison, he did not give up or grow bitter. He continued to serve others and earned the trust of the prison keeper. *"But the Lord was with Joseph and showed him mercy, and He gave him favor in the sight of the keeper of the prison... whatever he did, the Lord made it prosper."* —Genesis 39:21–23, NKJV)

One day, two of Pharaoh's servants had dreams, and Joseph said, *"Do not interpretations belong to God? Tell them to me, please."* (Genesis 40:8, NKJV) That small act of service opened the door to his future promotion.

Jesus teaches us, *"He who is faithful in what is least is faithful also in much."* (Luke 16:10, NKJV) When we are faithful with little, God trusts us with more.

Waiting with Purpose

Waiting isn't always easy, but it has meaning. Joseph waited many years before his breakthrough came, but he didn't waste that time. He learned, served, and trusted God through it all. *"Wait on the Lord; be of good courage, and He shall strengthen your heart; wait, I say, on the Lord!"* (Psalm 27:14, NKJV)

Joseph also worked hard, even in difficult places. *"And whatever you do, do it heartily, as to the Lord and not to men."* (Colossians 3:23, NKJV) God uses every season to teach us, grow us, and prepare us for what comes next.

Knowing When to Step Out

God's timing is perfect. Joseph didn't rush or try to force his way out of prison. He waited for God's open door. When Pharaoh had a dream, Joseph was ready. *"To everything there is a season, a time for every purpose under heaven."* (Ecclesiastes 3:1, NKJV)

While we wait, we grow. *"And let us not grow weary while doing good, for in due season we shall reap if we do not lose heart."* (Galatians 6:9, NKJV) God always rewards those who stay faithful through the process.

The Process of Dying to Self

Before Joseph could step into his destiny, he had to die to self—letting go of pride, selfish ambition, and the desire to be recognized. True growth begins in surrender. As Jesus said, *"Listen carefully: Unless a grain of wheat is buried in the ground, dead to the world, it is never any more than a grain of wheat. But if it is buried, it sprouts and reproduces itself many times over."* —John 12:24 (MSG) Though the process may feel painful, it leads to new life, inner strength, and lasting fruitfulness.

Learning in the Hidden Season

Every leader must learn from their hidden season. Your current struggles, delays, or unnoticed work are not signs of failure but steps in God's preparation for future glory. Joseph's story reminds us that God doesn't forget or waste anything.

Even when no one else sees what you're doing, God sees and remembers. He's shaping your character, strengthening your heart, and preparing you for what's next. Stay faithful. Your season of fruitfulness is coming.

Reflection Questions

1. Are you in a season of quiet or waiting? How might God be using this time to grow you?

2. How has God been shaping your character, patience, or faith in this hidden season?

3. Are there areas where you've been resisting stillness instead of trusting God's timing?

Faith Steps

- **Pray for Clarity:** Ask God to show you what He is building in you during this quiet season and to help you trust His process.

- **Recognize Growth:** Identify one area—like patience, humility, or faith—where you've grown recently, even without big changes around you.

- **Embrace Stillness:** Set aside quiet time each day to reflect, pray, or worship. Let God use this space to strengthen and renew you.

Scripture Meditation

"But those who wait on the Lord shall renew their strength; they shall mount up with wings life eagles, they shall run and not be weary, they shall walk and not faint." — Isaiah 40:31 (NKJV)

Meditation Reflection

Hidden seasons can be frustrating. We may feel overlooked, forgotten, or stuck. But in God's eyes, these are seasons of preparation, not punishment. Joseph spent years in prison and slavery before stepping into leadership—but those quiet years weren't wasted. God used them to grow Joseph's trust, patience, and wisdom.

Isaiah 40:31 reminds us that waiting on God brings strength. Waiting doesn't mean doing nothing—it means trusting, listening, and growing deeper in faith. When you feel stuck or unseen, remember: God is doing a deep work in you.

Even when it seems like nothing is happening on the outside, God is working on the inside—shaping your heart, refining your character, and preparing you for what's next. Just like a seed planted in the ground, your growth may be hidden for a time, but in God's perfect season, it will bear fruit.

Key Meditation Points

- **Hidden Seasons Are for Growth:** Like Joseph, your quiet seasons are building the strength and wisdom needed for your future calling.

- **Stillness Is Preparation, Not Delay:** God uses silence and stillness to deepen your roots in Him. This time matters more than you may realize.

- **Faithfulness Leads to Fruitfulness:** When you stay faithful in small things, God prepares you for greater opportunities ahead.

Prayer for Growth in Hidden Seasons

Dear God,
Thank You for this season of stillness. Even when I feel unseen, I trust that You are working behind the scenes. Help me to be faithful, even when it's quiet. Grow my character and help me walk in patience, faith, and humility. When I feel discouraged, remind me that You are near. Show me how to use this time wisely and prepare my heart for the things You have ahead. Like Joseph, help me trust Your timing and stay committed to the work You've placed in front of me today.
I believe You are making me stronger, even when I can't see it. I surrender this season to You and trust that You're using it for my good and Your glory. In Jesus' name, Amen.

PART 2

GROWING AS A LEADER AND BUSINESS BUILDER

Focus: Gaining tools and strategies to grow in leadership, faith, and marketplace success.

CHAPTER 6

SERVING BEFORE LEADING — FAITHFULNESS IN SMALL THINGS

"So Joseph found favor in his sight, and served him. Then he made him overseer of his house, and all that he had he put under his authority. So it was, from the time that he had made him overseer of his house and all that he had, that the Lord blessed the Egyptian's house for Joseph's sake; and the blessing of the Lord was on all that he had in the house and in the field." —Genesis 39:4–5 (NKJV)

Before you can lead others, you must first learn to serve. In God's Kingdom, leadership doesn't begin with titles or attention. It begins in the quiet places—where no one sees but God. Joseph didn't start as Egypt's leader. He started by serving faithfully, even in hard and lonely situations.

God is watching how we handle the small things. When we show we can be trusted, He prepares us for more. *"It is required in stewards that one be found faithful"* (1 Corinthians 4:2, NKJV). This means we're managers of what belongs to God—our time, gifts, and even our attitude in the waiting. Joseph's story reminds us that faithfulness always comes before promotion.

Serving Is Part of God's Original Design

God created work and responsibility as part of our purpose. When Adam was placed in the garden, God gave him a job—to tend and care for it. *Genesis 2:15* shows us that God values stewardship from the beginning. It's not about being perfect but about showing up with care and consistency.

Whether it's helping around the house, showing up on time, or doing your schoolwork with a good heart, these everyday things matter. You don't need a spotlight to be important in God's eyes. When you serve well in small ways, you're actually growing into the kind of leader God can use.

Joseph in Potiphar's House

When Joseph was sold as a slave, his situation was painful. But he didn't let bitterness or fear stop him from doing his best. He worked faithfully in Potiphar's house, showing integrity in everything he did. As a result, Potiphar saw something different in him.

Genesis 39:4–6 tells us that Potiphar gave Joseph full responsibility for his house. Joseph didn't ask for a high position—it was his faithfulness that opened the door. When we give our best, even when it's hard, God honors that work, and others take notice.

Serving in Hard Places

Sometimes serving means doing our best in places we don't like. For Joseph, that meant prison. He had done nothing wrong, but he was still thrown behind bars. Even there, he didn't complain or give up. He stayed faithful and worked hard.

The prison guard trusted Joseph so much that he put him in charge. Genesis 39:21–23 says that God gave Joseph favor and made everything he touched successful. This reminds us that God can use every place—even the painful ones—to prepare us for something greater.

Helping Someone Else's Dream

Before Joseph saw his own dream come true, he helped others with theirs. He managed Potiphar's house, served the prison warden, and even interpreted dreams for fellow prisoners. He was always looking for ways to serve and support others.

Proverbs 27:18 teaches, *"Whoever keeps the fig tree will eat its fruit."* That means when you help someone else grow, you grow too. Joseph's willingness to serve others showed that he was ready for greater responsibility. God saw his heart, and the right opportunity came at the perfect time.

Why Humility, Excellence, and Hard Work Matter

Joseph could have acted prideful or bitter because of his past. But he didn't. He stayed humble and gave his best in every situation. He trusted that God saw his work, even when people overlooked him. *James 4:10* reminds us, *"Humble yourselves in the sight of the Lord, and He will lift you up."*

Real leadership doesn't chase recognition—it builds trust through steady, excellent work. Joseph's story teaches us to stay faithful, even when it feels like nothing is changing. That kind of leadership always stands out, and God rewards it in His time.

Learning from Mistakes

No one gets it right all the time. Leaders will make mistakes, but what matters is how we respond. Joseph experienced setbacks, but he didn't let failure define him. He stayed focused and allowed God to keep shaping his heart.

Proverbs 24:16 says, *"A righteous person may fall seven times and rise again."* That means even when we mess up, we can rise stronger if we keep trusting God. Learning from our mistakes, growing in grace, and staying faithful is what prepares us to lead well.

Reflection Questions

1. In what small roles or tasks is God teaching you to be faithful right now?

2. How can you shift your mindset to see this season of preparation as part of God's bigger plan?

3. What is one small act of obedience you can commit to today that honors God?

Faith Steps

- **Choose One Area of Excellence:** Pick one small area in your work or relationships to improve this week. Ask God to help you give your best in it.

- **Remember Your Growth:** Think back to a time when God used a small beginning to prepare you for something bigger. Write down what you learned.

- **Pray for a Servant's Heart:** Ask God to fill your heart with patience, humility, and joy as you serve in your current season.

Scripture Meditation

"Do not despise these small beginnings, for the Lord rejoices to see the work begin, to see the plumb line in Zerubbabel's hand." — Zechariah 4:10 (NLT)

Meditation Reflection

Sometimes it's easy to feel like the work we're doing doesn't matter—especially if it's behind the scenes or feels small. But God sees it all. Joseph started by managing someone else's house and then a prison. These small roles shaped him for the big job of leading a nation.

God delights in our faithfulness, even in the little things. Whether you're helping someone else succeed, working a quiet job, or starting something new, it's not small to Him. These are training grounds for the future.

Just like a seed planted in the soil, your efforts may be hidden for now, but they're growing something deep. God uses these humble beginnings to prepare your heart, sharpen your skills, and shape your character. Don't rush the process—this season matters.

Key Meditation Points

- **Small Things Matter to God:** Your daily efforts, no matter how small, are part of His plan and bring Him joy.

- **Faithfulness Builds Leadership:** Like Joseph, staying diligent in your current season prepares you for greater influence later.

- **God Honors a Humble Heart:** Serving with integrity, even when no one sees it, brings God's favor and aligns you with His purpose.

Prayer for Faithfulness in Small Beginnings

Dear God,
Thank You for reminding me that small beginnings have great value in Your Kingdom. Help me to stay faithful in this season, even when I feel unnoticed or discouraged.

Teach me to give my best in the little things. Fill my heart with humility, patience, and a desire to serve well. As I do my work, may it reflect Your love and bring You glory.

I trust that You are using every step—even the quiet ones—to prepare me for what's ahead. Shape me into the leader You've called me to be.

In Jesus' name, Amen.

CHAPTER 7

INTEGRITY AND INFLUENCE — THE FOUNDATION OF LASTING SUCCESS

"The integrity of the upright will guide them, But the perversity of the unfaithful will destroy them."—Proverbs 11:3 (NKJV)

True leadership is built on integrity. That means doing what is right even when no one is watching. Joseph's story shows us how powerful integrity can be. He didn't become a leader just because he was smart or talented.

He became a leader because people could trust him. God could trust him too. Integrity means your actions match your values. *"The integrity of the upright will guide them, but the perversity of the unfaithful will destroy them."* (Proverbs 11:3, NKJV)

Joseph's Test of Integrity

One of the biggest tests in Joseph's life came when Potiphar's wife tried to tempt him. She pressured him over and over, but Joseph stayed faithful to God.

> *And it came to pass after these things that his master's wife cast longing eyes on Joseph, and she said, "Lie with me." But he refused and said to his master's wife, "Look, my master does not know what is with me in the house, and he has committed all that he has to my hand. There is no one greater in this house than I, nor has he kept back anything from me but you, because you are his wife. How then can I do this great wickedness, and sin against God?" So it was, as she spoke to Joseph day by day, that he did not heed her, to lie with her or to be with her."* — Genesis 39:7–10, NKJV

He chose to honor God, even though it meant trouble was coming.

Even though Joseph did the right thing, he was falsely accused and thrown into prison. That didn't stop him from holding on to what was right. He didn't give up or grow bitter. *"Still he holds fast to his integrity, although you incited Me against him, to destroy him without cause."* (Job 2:3, NKJV)

Joseph's choice came with a cost, but it also came with a reward. He stayed true to God and didn't compromise. God continued to work behind the scenes. That's what integrity does—it keeps you on the right path even in unfair situations.

Why Integrity Builds Trust

People follow leaders they can trust. Trust is not built in one day—it's built through your choices every day. When people see that you're truthful, they'll want to follow you. *"He who walks with integrity walks securely, but he who perverts his ways will become known."* (Proverbs 10:9, NKJV)

Integrity brings peace to your heart. You don't have to live in fear of getting caught or being fake. You're walking in truth and doing what's right. *"A good name is to be chosen rather than great riches, loving favor rather than silver and gold."* (Proverbs 22:1, NKJV)

When you live with honesty and kindness, others notice. They see that you don't gossip or hurt people to get ahead. Your leadership becomes stronger because people know you're real. *"He who walks uprightly, and works righteousness, and speaks the truth in his heart; He who does not backbite with his tongue, nor does evil to his neighbor, nor does he take up a reproach against his friend."* (Psalm 15:2–3, NKJV)

Leading with Character

Leadership isn't just about being good at something—it's about being someone others can count on. Character shows up when you make tough choices for the right reasons. It's built through the hard times, not just the easy ones. *"And not only that, but we also glory in tribulations, knowing that tribulation produces perseverance; and perseverance, character; and character, hope."* (Romans 5:3–4, NKJV)

Joseph led with character whether he was in a house, prison, or palace. He didn't change his values based on where he was. That kind of consistency made him stand out. He was trustworthy in small things first.

"He who is faithful in what is least is faithful also in much; and he who is unjust in what is least is unjust also in much." (Luke 16:10, NKJV) God promotes leaders who stay faithful behind the scenes. He sees the little things that others overlook.

Handling Pressure Without Compromise

Every leader faces moments of pressure. Those moments test what you're really made of. Will you take shortcuts? Or will you trust God and do what's right?

Joseph didn't let fear or pressure change who he was. He knew that God was with him through it all. *"Fear not, for I am with you; be not dismayed, for I am your God. I will strengthen you, Yes, I will help you, I will uphold you with My righteous right hand."* (Isaiah 41:10, NKJV)

Choosing integrity invites God's strength. It reminds us that we don't have to face pressure alone. When we do the right thing, God steps in to help us stand strong. Integrity under pressure makes you an even stronger leader.

Lasting Influence Comes from Integrity

Joseph's influence wasn't just about success—it was about trust. He didn't ask for power, but because of his character, God placed him in a powerful position. *"Then Pharaoh said to Joseph, 'Inasmuch as God has shown you all this, there is no one as discerning and wise as you.'"* (Genesis 41:39, NKJV)

Integrity opens doors you could never open on your own. It leads to relationships, promotions, and the chance to help others. *"He who follows righteousness and mercy finds life, righteousness, and honor."* (Proverbs 21:21, NKJV)

God uses leaders who are faithful, honest, and kind. That kind of leadership brings peace to others too. *"The work of righteousness will be peace, and the effect of righteousness, quietness and assurance forever."* (Isaiah 32:17, NKJV)

Reflection Questions

1. How can you show integrity in your role, relationships, or leadership this week?

2. Are there any areas where you feel tempted to compromise? How can you stand firm instead?

3. How can your example of integrity encourage others around you?

Faith Steps

- **Choose an Area for Growth:** Think of one part of your life—work, school, or relationships—where you can grow in honesty and integrity.

- **Make a Courageous Choice:** This week, commit to making a decision that reflects God's truth, even if it's hard.

- **Ask God for Strength:** Pray for wisdom and boldness to do what's right, especially when it feels easier to stay quiet or give in.

Scripture Meditation

"Whoever walks in integrity walks securely, but whoever takes crooked paths will be found out." — Proverbs 10:9 (NIV)

Meditation Reflection

Integrity means doing what's right—even when no one is watching. Joseph modeled this kind of integrity when he refused to sin, even though it would've been easier and safer to give in. His choice cost him prison, but it also positioned him for God's favor.
God cares deeply about our character. He sees our decisions, our private thoughts, and the motives behind our actions. Integrity builds trust with others and brings peace in our own hearts. We don't have to live with guilt or fear when we walk in truth.

Proverbs 10:9 says those who walk in integrity walk securely. That means we can live without fear of being "found out" because we've chosen honesty from the start. Choosing integrity may not always bring quick rewards—but it builds a strong foundation that God can bless.

In moments of pressure or temptation, pause and ask, "What would honor God?" Your decision may require sacrifice, but it will lead to long-term peace, growth, and favor. Like Joseph, when you choose righteousness, you step into God's greater plan for your life.

Key Meditation Points

- **Integrity Builds Confidence:** Walking in truth gives peace and security. You don't have to hide when you've done what's right.

- **God Honors Your Stand:** Just like Joseph, when you choose righteousness over ease, God will reward your faithfulness.

- **Your Integrity Influences Others:** Your honest choices set an example and open the door for greater impact.

Prayer for Integrity and Strength

Dear God,
Thank You for showing me the power of integrity through Joseph's story. Help me choose truth, even when it's hard. Give me courage to do what's right and wisdom to know how to lead with honesty and strength.
When I feel pressure to compromise, remind me that You see every decision and reward those who trust in You. Shape my heart to reflect Your character, and let my choices inspire others to walk in Your ways.
I want my life to be built on truth and guided by Your Spirit. Help me be faithful in every moment, trusting that You are leading me toward Your best.
In Jesus' name, Amen.

CHAPTER 8

THRIVING IN THE WILDERNESS — GROWING WHILE YOU WAIT

"And you shall remember that the Lord your God led you all the way these forty years in the wilderness, to humble you and test you, to know what was in your heart, whether you would keep His commandments or not. So He humbled you, allowed you to hunger, and fed you with manna which you did not know nor did your fathers know, that He might make you know that man shall not live by bread alone; but man lives by every word that proceeds from the mouth of the Lord."— Deuteronomy 8:2–3 (NKJV)

Waiting can feel really hard. Sometimes it seems like nothing is happening and everyone has forgotten you. But in God's Kingdom, waiting isn't wasted—it's a time of preparation. God often uses quiet and hidden seasons to grow our faith, shape our hearts, and get us ready for something greater.

Joseph's time in prison was a long season of waiting. People may have forgotten him, but God never did. While it seemed like life had paused,

Joseph stayed faithful to what was in front of him. He kept serving others and using his gifts, trusting that God had not forgotten his dreams.

Growing in Hard Places

Joseph had every reason to be discouraged. He had helped the king's butler in prison, but when the butler got out, *"the chief butler did not remember Joseph but forgot him." — Genesis 40:23 (NKJV)* That must have hurt deeply, especially since Joseph had done the right thing. But he didn't let that disappointment stop him from trusting God.

Hard seasons are often where we grow the most. It might feel like nothing is changing on the outside, but inside, God is building strength and maturity. Like roots growing underground, we're being made stronger for what's coming. *"My brethren, count it all joy when you fall into various trials, knowing that the testing of your faith produces patience. But let patience have its perfect work, that you may be perfect and complete, lacking nothing." — James 1:2–4 (NKJV)*

Even though we don't enjoy the hard moments, they're important. God is preparing us for future responsibility. Joseph didn't know what would happen next, but he stayed committed to doing what was right. That kind of faith grows deep when we let God work through our waiting.

Dying to Self Before Stepping into Purpose

Before Joseph could lead a nation, he had to let go of pride, control, and personal timing. In other words, he had to "die to self"—to trust God's way more than his own. It's not easy to do, but it's necessary if we want to fulfill God's calling.

Jesus explained this truth using a seed as a picture: *"Unless a grain of wheat falls into the ground and dies, it remains alone. But if it dies, it produces much grain." — John 12:24 (NKJV)* Like that seed, Joseph had to be buried in hiddenness before he could grow into his calling. He learned to live for God's purpose instead of his own comfort.

Letting go of our own plans makes room for God's better ones. Joseph didn't need a spotlight—he focused on growing in faith and character. That's what made him ready when his moment came. When we surrender, God transforms us from the inside out.

The Wilderness Is a Training Ground

Many people think the wilderness is a place of punishment, but it's actually a place of preparation. God led His people through the desert to get them ready for the Promised Land. *"For You, O God, have tested us; You have refined us as silver is refined."* —*Psalm 66:10 (NKJV)* That refining process still happens today.

The wilderness teaches us to trust God more than we trust ourselves. It helps us learn obedience and patience. *"And you shall remember that the Lord your God led you all the way... to humble you and test you, to know what was in your heart."* —*Deuteronomy 8:2 (NKJV)* God wanted their hearts to be prepared before giving them more responsibility.

Joseph's wilderness wasn't a desert, but it was still dry and lonely. His time in prison tested his trust in God. But because he didn't give up, his heart was ready when promotion came. God uses these seasons to grow us—not to punish us, but to prepare us.

Serving While You Wait

One of the most powerful things you can do while waiting is serve. That's what Joseph did. In prison, he looked for ways to help others—even though he was going through his own challenges. He didn't wait for a better stage—he used the one he had.

Serving helps us stay focused on others, not just ourselves. It also allows our gifts to grow in real-life situations. *"A man's gift makes room for him, and brings him before great men." —Proverbs 18:16 (NKJV)* When we use our gifts to serve others, we're preparing for what's ahead.

Joseph's service opened the door to his next assignment. He interpreted dreams for fellow prisoners, and that skill later helped him interpret Pharaoh's dream. That's the power of faithfulness—what you do in private often leads to public influence later.

Trusting God's Timing

It's hard to be patient, especially when you feel ready for more. But God's timing is never too early or too late. He sees the whole picture, and He knows when the time is right. *"Wait on the Lord; be of good courage, and He shall strengthen your heart; Wait, I say, on the Lord!" —Psalm 27:14 (NKJV)*

Joseph waited for years before anything changed. It might have looked like nothing was happening, but God was setting everything in motion behind the scenes. When Pharaoh finally had a dream, Joseph was called out of prison and into leadership. That shift happened in a single day—but it was built on years of faithfulness.

Trusting God means we believe His plan is better than ours. Waiting is not doing nothing—it's preparing with faith. When you trust His timing, He will open the right doors at the right time. Stay faithful, stay focused, and know that your moment is coming.

Reflection Questions

1. What is God teaching you during your current season of waiting?

2. Are there areas of your life where you need to trust God's timing more fully?

3. How can you use your gifts right now to serve others, even if no one sees it?

Faith Steps

- **Grow Where You Are:** Choose one area—like your skills, spiritual life, or relationships—to develop while you wait. Ask God to help you grow in it this week.

- **Use Your Gifts Quietly:** Find a way to serve others with your talents, even in small or behind-the-scenes ways.

- **Trust the Process:** When you feel frustrated or tired, remind yourself that God's timing is perfect, and He is preparing you for something greater.

Scripture Meditation

> "But those who wait on the Lord shall renew their strength; they shall mount up with wings like eagles, they shall run and not be weary, they shall walk and not faint." — Isaiah 40:31 (NKJV)

Meditation Reflection

Waiting can be hard. It's easy to feel like nothing is happening or that your time is being wasted. But in God's Kingdom, waiting seasons are full of purpose. Just like Joseph, who waited in slavery and prison before becoming a leader in Egypt, God is using your quiet season to prepare you for something greater.

While Joseph was waiting, God was shaping his heart, building his character, and training him to lead. Your waiting season is not a delay—it's development. God may be teaching you patience, building resilience, or showing you how to trust Him more deeply.

Isaiah 40:31 reminds us that waiting on the Lord gives us strength. Waiting isn't sitting around doing nothing—it's staying faithful, growing, and trusting God to work things out in His perfect time. You don't have to have all the answers right now. Just stay obedient where you are, and God will open the right doors when the time is right.

Key Meditation Points

- **Waiting Is Part of the Process:** God uses delays to shape our hearts, strengthen our faith, and prepare us for what's next.

- **Faithfulness Prepares You for Promotion:** Like Joseph, staying diligent in small places prepares you for future leadership.

- **God's Timing Is Always Right:** Even when it feels slow, God is never late. Trust that He is working behind the scenes.

Prayer for Growth and Trust

Dear God,
Thank You for using this waiting season to shape me. Help me see it not as a pause but as a time to grow stronger, wiser, and more faithful. When I feel discouraged or forgotten, remind me that You are still working.
Give me patience and trust. Help me stay focused and serve well, even when no one sees. I believe that You are preparing me for something greater, and I choose to walk in faith until that time comes.
In Jesus' name, Amen.

CHAPTER 9

RECOGNIZING GOD MOMENTS — GETTING READY FOR OPPORTUNITY

"A man's gift makes room for him, and brings him before great men."—Proverbs 18:16 (NKJV)

When God opens a door, we need to be ready to walk through it. But that kind of readiness doesn't happen overnight. Joseph didn't go from prison to the palace in one day. He spent years learning, growing, and preparing in quiet places so he could step into leadership when the time was right.

Proverbs 16:9 reminds us, *"A man's heart plans his way, but the Lord directs his steps."* Even if you don't understand your journey, trust that God is leading you on purpose. You may have your own ideas, but God sees the whole picture. He is guiding you toward your assignment—even in the hard seasons.

Be Ready Before the Opportunity Comes

God often begins preparing us before we even know what He's preparing us for. Joseph didn't waste his time in slavery or prison. He learned how to manage people, solve problems, and stay faithful in pressure-filled places. So when Pharaoh needed someone wise and trustworthy, Joseph was ready.

Joseph gave all credit to God for the wisdom he had. His response to Pharaoh in Genesis 41:16 was this: *"It is not in me; God will give Pharaoh an answer of peace."* His humility showed that his heart was ready to lead. Years of hidden faithfulness prepared him for a public opportunity.

Proverbs 3:5–6 says, *"Trust in the Lord with all your heart, and lean not on your own understanding; in all your ways acknowledge Him, and He shall direct your paths."* God's preparation often feels hidden, but it's never wasted. Even if others don't notice, God is shaping you for the doors He's going to open.

Skills That Open Doors

Joseph didn't just interpret dreams—he developed leadership skills by serving faithfully in difficult places. In Potiphar's house, he learned how to oversee work. In prison, he managed people with fairness and care. These skills helped him govern an entire nation with wisdom and excellence.

God gives us spiritual gifts, but He also expects us to grow through practice. *Ephesians 2:10* reminds us, *"For we are His workmanship, created in Christ Jesus for good works, which God prepared beforehand that we should walk in them."* Your talents were given for a purpose—and training makes them stronger.

When we use our gifts for good and stay teachable, we grow in influence. God can do big things with someone who gives Him their best every day. *Proverbs 4:7* says, *"Wisdom is the principal thing; therefore get wisdom. And in all your getting, get understanding."* Learning never stops in the Kingdom.

Stay Faithful in Small Things

Joseph didn't wait to be in the palace to give his best. He served in Potiphar's house and then in prison with excellence and heart. He took care of others, showed kindness, and stayed disciplined even when no one was watching. That's how trust is built—by being faithful in small places.

Jesus set this example too. *Mark 10:45* says, *"For even the Son of Man did not come to be served, but to serve, and to give His life a ransom for many."* If Jesus served humbly, then we are called to do the same. Great leaders begin as great servants.

When we work with excellence in hidden places, God gets glory. *Luke 16:10* tells us, *"He who is faithful in what is least is faithful also in much."* If we're responsible with the small things, God can trust us with more.

Discern God's Timing

Joseph didn't force his way to the top. He waited for the right moment, and when Pharaoh called for him, he was ready. Not every open door is from God, so we must pray for wisdom to know which opportunities to take. God's voice and peace will always lead the way.

Proverbs 11:14 reminds us, *"Where there is no counsel, the people fall; but in the multitude of counselors there is safety."* Wise leaders surround themselves with godly mentors and seek prayerful advice. They don't rush. They listen and wait on God's confirmation.

When it's God's time, things happen quickly. But while you wait, stay focused and grow. *Isaiah 41:10* encourages us: *"Fear not, for I am with you; be not dismayed, for I am your God. I will strengthen you, yes, I will help you, I will uphold you with My righteous right hand."* God's timing is always right—and so is His help.

Build a Kingdom Mindset

Joseph used his influence to serve others, not himself. He didn't become arrogant with power or seek revenge. Instead, he used his position to help people, save lives, and restore relationships. That's what a Kingdom mindset looks like in action.

Philippians 2:5 says, *"Let this mind be in you which was also in Christ Jesus."* Jesus lived to serve and love, even when it was hard. When we lead with His mindset, our decisions look different. We choose compassion, humility, and justice over pride.

Your gifts were never just for your success—they were meant to bless others. When you lead with a Kingdom heart, you point people to Jesus. And in doing so, you become the kind of leader who changes the world.

Reflection Questions

1. How can you prepare now for the opportunities God may bring in the future?

2. Are there skills or habits you need to grow while waiting for God's timing?

3. What does it look like to stay faithful and diligent in the season you're in right now?

Faith Steps

- **Strengthen One Area:** Choose one part of your life—like prayer, leadership, or time management—to grow in this week.

- **Pray for Discernment:** Ask God to help you notice divine opportunities and give you the courage to walk through the right doors.

- **Stay Faithful Now:** Keep giving your best to the roles and responsibilities you already have, trusting that they're part of your preparation.

Scripture Meditation

"I know your works. See, I have set before you an open door, and no one can shut it; for you have a little strength, have kept My word, and have not denied My name." — Revelation 3:8 (NKJV)

Meditation Reflection

God is the One who opens doors—and when He opens one, no one can shut it. That's a powerful truth. Even when you feel small or unqualified, God knows your heart and your faithfulness. He's not looking for perfection—He's looking for readiness.

Joseph's story reminds us that big moments often follow seasons of quiet preparation. Before standing before Pharaoh, Joseph served faithfully in Potiphar's house and prison. He didn't know when his opportunity would come, but he stayed ready. When the time came, he stepped up with wisdom and courage.

The same is true for you. The season you're in right now matters. Every skill you sharpen, every act of obedience, and every time you stay faithful in small things, you're building a strong foundation for future influence.

Don't be discouraged if things seem slow. God is preparing you behind the scenes. When the right door opens, you won't need to force it—you'll be ready to walk through it with confidence because God has equipped you for it.

Key Meditation Points

- **God Opens Doors in His Timing:** Trust that when the time is right, God will open the right opportunities—and no one can close what He has set before you.

- **Preparation Builds Readiness:** Your current season is shaping you. Use this time to grow your faith, character, and skills.

- **Stay Faithful in the Now:** Even small tasks matter. Your diligence today is preparing you for influence tomorrow.

Prayer for Preparation and Opportunity

Dear God,
Thank You for every season of preparation. Help me trust that You are leading me, even when I don't see everything clearly. Grow my heart to be faithful, focused, and ready for the doors You will open.
Give me wisdom to recognize divine opportunities and courage to walk through them when the time comes. Help me stay committed to serving well in this season, knowing You are shaping me for greater purpose.
I surrender my timeline and trust Your plan. Use me for Your glory and prepare me for all You've called me to do.
In Jesus' name, Amen.

CHAPTER 10

THE ENTREPRENEUR'S SPIRIT—BUILDING WITH VISION AND FAITH

"And you shall remember the Lord your God, for it is He who gives you power to get wealth, that He may establish His covenant which He swore to your fathers, as it is this day."
—Deuteronomy 8:18 (NKJV)

Being an entrepreneur takes more than good ideas or wanting to make money. True Kingdom entrepreneurship begins with purpose. It's about using your gifts to solve problems, bless others, and bring glory to God. Joseph's story reminds us that success comes from leading with both vision and faith.

"The plans of the diligent lead surely to plenty, but those of everyone who is hasty, surely to poverty." (Proverbs 21:5) When we plan carefully with God's help, we can build something that lasts and blesses others. God gave Joseph wisdom to manage resources during a famine. He didn't just save Egypt—he created

systems that helped entire nations survive. This kind of impact starts with a heart that listens to God's plan.

When God gives you a dream, it might seem impossible at first. But God is the one who makes a way when it seems there is no way. *Jesus said, "With men this is impossible, but with God all things are possible."* (Matthew 19:26) Don't let fear stop you from building what God has placed in your heart.

What Is Kingdom Entrepreneurship?

In the world, business often focuses on profit and personal gain. But in God's Kingdom, business is about purpose. It's about using your gifts to serve others, meet needs, and bring glory to God. Kingdom entrepreneurs trust God for direction and believe that He provides everything they need to succeed.

Joseph was more than a dreamer—he was a planner, a problem-solver, and a leader. He saw a big problem coming and, with God's help, came up with a plan to save Egypt and many other nations. That's what a Kingdom entrepreneur does—he or she looks ahead, prays, listens to God, and builds solutions.

Building Beyond Comfort Zones

To grow in your calling, you'll need to step out of your comfort zone. God often stretches us so we can grow into who He created us to be. Joseph didn't stay in a safe place—he went from a prison to a palace, from being forgotten to being promoted. Each step required courage, faith, and obedience.

Ephesians 3:20 reminds us, *"Now to Him who is able to do exceedingly abundantly above all that we ask or think."* When we trust God and walk in faith, He does more than we could ever imagine.

What Is Kingdom Economy?

God's way of handling money and resources is different from the world's way. In the Kingdom, we don't rely only on jobs or bank accounts—we trust God as our Provider. He owns everything. Our job is to manage what He gives us with wisdom, generosity, and faith.

In 2 Corinthians 9:8, Paul writes, "And God is able to make all grace abound toward you… that you may have an abundance for every good work." God blesses us so we can bless others. We are not owners—we are stewards.

Joseph's Strategy: A Model for Us

When Pharaoh had troubling dreams about a coming famine, Joseph stepped in with a plan. He didn't just give advice—he gave a clear solution. Joseph said to store grain during the good years so there would be food during the famine. Pharaoh agreed, and Egypt was saved.

Genesis 41:48-49 says Joseph "gathered up all the food of the seven years… and laid up the food in the cities." His wisdom helped Egypt survive and bless others. That's what great entrepreneurs do—they prepare, plan, and use resources wisely.

Starting and Leading with Faith

If you want to start a business or lead something new, begin with faith. Trust God to show you the steps. Ask for His wisdom. Proverbs 3:5-6 tells us, *"Trust in the Lord with all your heart, and lean not on your own understanding."*

Faith-driven entrepreneurs don't just build for success—they build for purpose. They make decisions that honor God. They treat people fairly. They give generously. And when times get hard, they don't give up—they lean into God's promises.

Colossians 3:23 says, *"Whatever you do, do it heartily, as to the Lord and not to men."* This means your work—whether in a business, school, or ministry—can be worship when done with the right heart.

Business as a Way to Shine God's Light

Business isn't just about making money—it's a way to influence people for good. A God-centered business can bring hope, jobs, healing, and truth to communities. Jesus said in Matthew 5:16, *"Let your light so shine before men, that they may see your good works and glorify your Father in heaven."*

Like Joseph, we can use our influence to bless others. Whether you're mentoring someone, hiring fairly, or giving to a local need, you are expanding God's Kingdom.

Reflection Questions

1. How can you use your business or leadership role to reflect Kingdom values?

2. What is one area of your business where you need to trust God's timing and guidance?

3. How can you help build a culture of honesty, generosity, and servant leadership in your workplace?

Faith Steps

- **Live Your Values:** Choose one way to practice Kingdom principles in your daily business decisions—like showing honesty, generosity, or grace.

- **Bless Someone Through Business:** Identify one person or group to support through your time, resources, or influence this week.

- **Pray Over Your Work:** Set time aside to pray over your business or career, asking God to lead you with wisdom and open the right doors.

Scripture Meditation

> *"And you shall remember the Lord your God, for it is He who gives you power to get wealth, that He may establish His covenant, which He swore to your fathers, as it is this day."*—Deuteronomy 8:18 (NKJV)

Meditation Reflection

Your business, influence, or career is not just about making money—it's about advancing God's Kingdom. Deuteronomy 8:18 reminds us that it's God who gives us the ability to succeed. He blesses us not just for our benefit, but so we can make a difference in the lives of others.

Joseph's life is a great example of Kingdom leadership. Even though he faced many hardships, he stayed faithful. When God placed him in leadership, he used his position to help others and protect his people. Joseph didn't chase power—he followed God's plan with integrity and wisdom.

The same is true for you. God wants to use your business or leadership to bless others and shine His light. This means leading with honesty, serving others, and making decisions that reflect God's heart. When you run your business with Kingdom values, you create a space where people feel respected, valued, and inspired.

Don't wait until you "make it big" to start living out your faith. Every small decision, every act of kindness, and every prayer over your business matters. Trust that God is building something through you that will last far beyond profits or platforms.

Key Meditation Points

- **God Is the Source:** Your success and resources come from God. He gives you the power to build, grow, and influence for His purpose.

- **Lead with Integrity and Compassion:** Faith-based leadership means being honest, generous, and caring for people—not just chasing results.

- **Kingdom Impact Starts Now:** You don't need a big stage to make a difference. Serving faithfully in small things creates lasting influence.

Prayer for Kingdom Business Leadership

Dear God,
Thank You for blessing me with vision, gifts, and opportunity. Help me to lead with integrity and to reflect Your love in everything I do. Remind me that my business is Yours, and I'm here to serve others through it.
Guide my decisions and help me trust You, even when things are uncertain. Teach me to bless others with what You've given me—whether it's my time, resources, or encouragement. Let my work reflect Your Kingdom values every day.
May my business bring hope, serve people well, and honor You in all things. In Jesus' name, Amen.

PART 3
LEADING WITH IMPACT AND BUILDING GOD'S KINGDOM

Focus: Putting your leadership into action and making a long-term difference through faith and strategy.

CHAPTER II

THE JOSEPH LEADERSHIP MODEL — LEADING WITH PURPOSE, WISDOM, AND KINGDOM POWER

"Then Pharaoh said to Joseph, 'Inasmuch as God has shown you all this, there is no one as discerning and wise as you. You shall be over my house, and all my people shall be ruled according to your word; only in regard to the throne will I be greater than you.'" —Genesis 41:39–40 (NKJV)

Joseph's journey from the prison to the palace is more than just a story of success. It's a powerful picture of how God shapes leaders through faithfulness, obedience, and character. Joseph didn't chase fame or position—he stayed close to God, used his gifts to serve others, and remained faithful during trials. His life gives us a powerful blueprint for how to lead in today's world.

In this fast-moving world, we need leaders who are rooted in godly character and filled with spiritual wisdom. That's what the Joseph Leadership Model is all about. It's not just for CEOs or pastors—it's for anyone called to lead in their family, church, business, school, or community. Joseph's life teaches us how to lead with strength, vision, and humility, no matter where we are placed.

What is a Mantal?

A *mantle* is a special calling or assignment from God that someone carries. In the Bible, a mantle was often a symbol of leadership or a role passed from one person to another, like when Elijah passed his prophetic mantle to Elisha. Today, we use the word to describe the spiritual responsibility or leadership role that God gives someone. When a person receives a mantle, it means God has chosen them for a unique purpose—to serve, lead, or influence others in a meaningful way. It's not just about position or title but about faithfully carrying out God's plan with integrity, strength, and humility.

Joseph carried a leadership mantle that came straight from God. It wasn't given by people or earned by ambition—it was developed through trials, tested in private, and revealed at the right time. His mantle gave him the strength to lead wisely, serve faithfully, and point others to God. This same kind of mantle is available today for leaders who are willing to grow, serve, and obey God in every area of life.

Joseph's Fourfold Leadership Mantle

Joseph carried a unique leadership calling—a "Fourfold Leadership Mantle." A mantle is a spiritual assignment from God. Joseph's mantle included:

The Fourfold Leadership Mantle of Joseph

Role	What It Means	Bible References
King	Joseph carried a royal identity. He used his position to help lead and bring God's rule wherever he went.	Revelation 1:6, Isaiah 33:22, Romans 5:17
Ruler	Joseph led with wisdom and fairness. He made decisions that helped people and kept things in order.	Genesis 1:26, Psalm 72:8, Romans 13:3
Priest	Joseph stayed close to God. He prayed, worshiped, and carried God's presence into every place he served.	Exodus 28:1, Hebrews 5:1, 1 Peter 2:9
Ambassador for Christ	Joseph represented God and His ways. He showed others what Heaven's love, truth, and leadership look like.	2 Corinthians 5:20, John 20:21

Each part of this mantle worked together in Joseph's life. He didn't just rule like a leader—he led like someone sent by God. He used wisdom to govern, faith to endure, and compassion to serve.

The Bible Confirms the Joseph Mantle

Joseph's leadership was not something he made up. It lines up with what Scripture says about how God calls His people to lead.

> *"To Him who loved us and washed us from our sins in His own blood, and has made us kings and priests to His God and Father, to Him be glory and dominion forever and ever. Amen."*
> — Revelation 1:5–6 (NKJV)

> *"Now then, we are ambassadors for Christ, as though God were pleading through us: we implore you on Christ's behalf, be reconciled to God."* — 2 Corinthians 5:20 (NKJV)

These verses show that God has made us kings (to lead), priests (to minister), and ambassadors (to represent Him). Joseph walked in all three roles, and today's Kingdom leaders are called to do the same.

The Spirit of Joseph

Joseph had a different spirit. He stayed faithful even when life was unfair. He trusted God when he was falsely accused. He waited patiently for God's timing.

> *"Then Pharaoh said to Joseph, 'Inasmuch as God has shown you all this, there is no one as discerning and wise as you. You shall be over my house, and all my people shall be ruled according to your word; only in regard to the throne will I be greater than you.'"* — Genesis 41:39–40 (NKJV)

Pharaoh saw God's wisdom in Joseph. Joseph didn't use his gifts to promote himself—he used them to serve others and honor God. That's what sets apart godly leaders today.

Walking in the Four Parts of Joseph's Mantle

1. Kingship: Leading with God-Given Identity

Joseph didn't need a crown to act like royalty. He knew who he was—a child of Abraham and a servant of God. Kingship means leading from a place of confidence in God's promises.

> *"I will make you a great nation; I will bless you and make your name great; and you shall be a blessing. I will bless those who bless you, and I will curse him who curses you; and in you all the families of the earth shall be blessed."* — *Genesis 12:2–3 (NKJV)*

Kingship is not about control—it's about influence. It means using your voice, gifts, and position to bring blessing, order, and justice.

2. Rulership: Governing with Wisdom

Joseph didn't just interpret Pharaoh's dream—he gave him a plan. He created systems, managed food storage, and saved millions of lives during the famine.

> *"You shall be over my house, and all my people shall be ruled according to your word; only in regard to the throne will I be greater than you."* — Genesis 41:40 (NKJV)

Rulership is about managing what God puts in your hands—whether it's a job, a team, a business, or a home. It's using godly wisdom to serve others and bring solutions.

3. Priesthood: Living Close to God

Joseph didn't preach sermons, but he lived close to God. He ran from sin, stayed pure, and always gave God the credit. Priesthood is about carrying God's presence wherever you go.

> *"But you are a chosen generation, a royal priesthood, a holy nation, His own special people, that you may proclaim the praises of Him who called you out of darkness into His marvelous light."* — 1 Peter 2:9 (NKJV)

A priestly leader prays, listens to God, and invites His wisdom into every part of life. Priesthood is about worshiping with your life—not just with your lips.

4. Ambassador of Christ: Representing Heaven

Joseph didn't hide his faith. Even in Egypt, he stood strong. He showed Pharaoh that true wisdom came from God, not from magicians or idols.

> *"Now then, we are ambassadors for Christ, as though God were pleading through us: we implore you on Christ's behalf, be reconciled to God."* — *2 Corinthians 5:20 (NKJV)*

As God's ambassador, you don't just talk about Jesus—you show people who He is. You bring Heaven's values—love, justice, and peace—into your workplace, school, or community.

Five Leadership Principles from Joseph's Life

1. Visionary Leadership

Joseph saw what was coming and helped Egypt prepare. When Pharaoh had a dream, Joseph offered insight and a plan.

> *"Now therefore, let Pharaoh select a discerning and wise man, and set him over the land of Egypt... Then that food shall be as a reserve for the land for the seven years of famine."* — *Genesis 41:33, 36 (NKJV)*

Visionary leaders look ahead. They don't just react—they plan, prepare, and make space for God to work.

2. Crisis Management

Joseph led Egypt through a national crisis. He didn't panic. He used wisdom, teamwork, and trust in God to lead well.

> "The famine was over all the face of the earth, and Joseph opened all the storehouses and sold to the Egyptians. And the famine became severe in the land of Egypt." — Genesis 41:56 (NKJV)

Crisis reveals character. Godly leaders remain calm, seek wisdom, and help others through storms.

3. Wealth Stewardship

Joseph stored up grain in times of plenty so Egypt wouldn't suffer in famine. He didn't waste blessings—he managed them wisely.

> "Joseph gathered very much grain, as the sand of the sea, until he stopped counting, for it was without number." — Genesis 41:49 (NKJV)

Wealth stewardship means handling resources with care—saving, giving, and spending with purpose.

4. Strategic Influence

Joseph didn't just manage things—he influenced people. Pharaoh trusted him because he saw something different in him.

> "And Pharaoh said to Joseph, 'See, I have set you over all the land of Egypt.'" — Genesis 41:41 (NKJV)

When you lead with God's wisdom, people take notice. Influence grows when you lead with humility and serve with excellence.

5. Kingdom Mindset

Even after all his pain, Joseph saw that God had a bigger purpose. He didn't stay bitter—he trusted God's plan.

> *"But as for you, you meant evil against me, but God meant it for good, in order to bring it about as it is this day, to save many people alive."* — Genesis 50:20 (NKJV)

Kingdom leaders keep their eyes on the bigger picture. They trust that God is always at work—even in hard times.

Reflection Questions

1. What leadership quality from Joseph's life can you apply to your own leadership today?

2. Are there any leadership challenges you're facing that require more trust in God's wisdom?

3. How can you lead with both confidence and humility in your current role?

Faith Steps

- **Choose a Leadership Trait to Practice:** Focus on one quality Joseph showed—like wisdom, forgiveness, or planning—and apply it in your leadership this week.

- **Pray for Wisdom:** Ask God for insight and clarity as you make decisions, big or small. Trust Him to guide your leadership journey.

- **Mentor Someone:** Reach out to someone you can support, encourage, or guide. Sharing what you've learned helps you grow too.

Scripture Meditation

"Then Pharaoh said to Joseph, 'Inasmuch as God has shown you all this, there is no one as discerning and wise as you. You shall be over my house, and all my people shall be ruled according to your word;
only in regard to the throne will I be greater than you.'"
— *Genesis 41:39–40 (NKJV)*

Meditation Reflection

Joseph didn't become a great leader overnight. He was shaped by years of trials, service, and trust in God. Even when he faced betrayal, prison, and false accusations, Joseph stayed faithful. And when the moment came, he was ready to lead with wisdom and strength. Pharaoh recognized that Joseph had something special—God's wisdom. Joseph didn't take credit; he stayed humble and gave God the glory. His leadership helped save nations and protect God's people.
Leadership isn't just about having power—it's about how you use it. Joseph used his influence to serve, solve problems, and help others. You can do the same. Whether you lead a team, a business, a ministry, or your family, you're called to lead with character, compassion, and courage.

God wants to guide your leadership. When you rely on Him, He'll give you the wisdom and strength you need—even in tough situations. Just like Joseph, your leadership can leave a lasting impact when it's rooted in faith and humility.

Key Meditation Points

- **God Gives Wisdom for Leadership:** Like Joseph, ask God for guidance daily—He promises to give wisdom freely (James 1:5).

- **Integrity Builds Trust:** Joseph stayed true to God even under pressure. Leading with honesty and fairness earns respect and favor.

- **Stay Humble and Serve:** Great leaders serve others. Joseph's success came because he led with humility and remembered that his position was from God.

Prayer for Wisdom and Leadership

Dear God,
Thank You for showing me the kind of leader You want me to be through Joseph's example. Help me lead with integrity, wisdom, and a humble heart. Remind me that every decision matters and that You are with me every step of the way.
When leadership is hard, give me strength. When I need answers, give me wisdom. Let my influence point others to You and reflect Your love.
I trust You to guide my leadership. Use me to bless others and to carry out the purpose You've given me.
In Jesus' name, Amen.

CHAPTER 12

THE TEST OF POWER — LEADING WITH WISDOM, HUMILITY, AND DISCERNMENT

> *"But the wisdom that is from above is first pure, then peaceable, gentle, willing to yield, full of mercy and good fruits, without partiality and without hypocrisy."* —James 3:17 (NKJV)

Joseph's promotion from the prison to the palace came with incredible responsibility. Pharaoh placed him second in command and gave him full authority over Egypt's economy.

> *"And Pharaoh said to Joseph, 'See, I have set you over all the land of Egypt.' Then Pharaoh took his signet ring off his hand and put it on Joseph's hand; and he clothed him in garments of fine linen and put a gold chain around his neck. And he had him ride in the second chariot which he had; and they cried out before him, 'Bow the knee!' So he set him over all the land of Egypt."* — Genesis 41:41–43 (NKJV)

But Joseph never used his power for selfish reasons.

Instead, he used his influence to serve others and solve problems during the famine. He created a food plan to save lives across many nations. Joseph's leadership wasn't about status—it was about service. He showed us that true success comes when we use our position to bless others, not ourselves.

Leading with Wisdom

Joseph didn't guess his way through leadership—he used wisdom from God. When Pharaoh had confusing dreams, Joseph didn't take credit for the interpretation. *"It is not in me; God will give Pharaoh an answer of peace"* (Genesis 41:16). Joseph's wisdom led to a national plan that kept Egypt and other nations from starving.

We are reminded in *Ecclesiastes 10:10, "If the ax is dull, and one does not sharpen the edge, then he must use more strength; but wisdom brings success."* Wisdom helps us work smarter, not just harder. And *Proverbs 9:10* teaches, *"The fear of the Lord is the beginning of wisdom, and the knowledge of the Holy One is understanding."* God gives wisdom to those who seek Him.

Leading with Humility

Even though Joseph became powerful, he stayed humble and kind. He never used his authority to harm his brothers or get revenge. He saw God's plan in his pain. *"But as for you, you meant evil against me; but God meant it for good, in order to bring it about as it is this day, to save many people alive"* (Genesis 50:20).

Joseph didn't let pride take root in his heart. His humility helped him lead with a clear mind and a pure heart. When we remember that all power belongs to God, we lead differently. *"Trust in the Lord with all your heart, and lean not on your own understanding; in all your ways acknowledge Him, and He shall direct your paths"* (Proverbs 3:5–6).

Leading with Discernment

Discernment means understanding the right thing to do and the right time to do it. Joseph showed discernment in how he handled Pharaoh, the famine, and even his own family. His decisions were thoughtful and prayerful. *"Search me, O God, and know my heart; try me, and know my anxieties; and see if there is any wicked way in me, and lead me in the way everlasting"* (Psalm 139:23–24).

Jesus reminded us of the importance of godly leadership by contrasting it with worldly power. *"You know that those who are considered rulers over the Gentiles lord it over them, and their great ones exercise authority over them. Yet it shall not be so among you; but whoever desires to become great among you shall be your servant."* — Mark 10:42–43 (NKJV) True leadership is not about being above others—it's about humbly lifting others up with wisdom, grace, and love.

Success Is a Test

Success reveals what's inside our hearts. Joseph passed the test of power because he didn't let his position change his character. Instead of becoming proud, he stayed faithful to God. *"Do not be conformed to this world, but be transformed by the renewing of your mind, that you may prove what is that good and acceptable and perfect will of God"* (Romans 12:2).

Joseph didn't let success distract him from God's purpose. He continued to lead with integrity and grace. When we're trusted with more, God expects us to be even more faithful. That's why *Luke 16:8* says, *"The sons of this world are more shrewd... than the sons of light,"* reminding us to be wise with our influence.

Stewardship Over Status

Joseph never acted like he owned Egypt—he acted like a steward. A steward manages something for someone else. That's how we should see our gifts, talents, and opportunities. *"When the righteous are in authority, the people rejoice; but when a wicked man rules, the people groan"* (Proverbs 29:2). God wants His people to lead with righteousness and wisdom.

Jesus set the ultimate example of servant leadership. *"For even the Son of Man did not come to be served, but to serve, and to give His life a ransom for many"* (Mark 10:45). Our leadership should reflect His heart. *"Wisdom is the principal thing; therefore get wisdom. And in all your getting, get understanding"* (Proverbs 4:7). Joseph led with wisdom, humility, and purpose—and so can you.

Reflection Questions

1. Are there areas in your leadership where pride or control has taken the lead?

2. How can you show humility, integrity, and compassion as your influence grows?

3. What's one recent decision where you need to invite God's wisdom to make sure it reflects His will?

Faith Steps

- **Let Go of Pride:** Identify one area where you're tempted to lead in your own strength. Surrender it to God and ask for His grace to lead with humility.

- **Seek Accountability:** Invite a trusted friend or mentor to speak into your leadership journey and help you stay grounded in godly values.

- **Reflect on Joseph's Humility:** Look at how Joseph gave credit to God and stayed compassionate. Choose one way this week to lead with the same attitude.

Scripture Meditation

"He has shown you, O man, what is good; and what does the Lord require of you but to do justly, to love mercy, and to walk humbly with your God?" — Micah 6:8 (NKJV)

Meditation Reflection

Success in leadership isn't just about reaching goals—it's about how you lead. Joseph was given great power, yet he stayed humble and faithful to God. He didn't take credit for his success. Instead, he pointed back to God as the source of his wisdom and favor.

Even though Joseph oversaw Egypt's wealth and influence, he never let power change his heart. He led with compassion, forgave his brothers, and honored God with every decision. That kind of leadership inspires others and creates lasting impact.

Micah 6:8 reminds us what God values in leaders—doing what's right, showing mercy, and walking humbly. This kind of leadership builds trust and reflects God's heart. Pride may try to creep in, especially as you gain success, but humility keeps your heart open to God's direction.

Leadership is a gift to be stewarded—not a position to be used for personal gain. The more you grow in influence, the more you must lean on God's wisdom. Let your leadership point others back to Him.

Key Meditation Points

- **Humility Keeps You Grounded:** Like Joseph, staying humble in success helps you serve others and honor God in every decision.

- **Leadership Is a Stewardship:** Your influence is not just for you—it's a chance to bless others and carry out God's purpose.

- **God's Wisdom Leads Well:** When you seek God's wisdom, He will help you lead with fairness, honesty, and compassion.

Prayer for Humility and Leadership

Dear God,
Thank You for Joseph's example of leading with humility and wisdom. Help me lead the same way—with honesty, kindness, and a heart that stays close to You. When pride tries to sneak in, remind me that everything I have comes from You.
Teach me to use my influence to serve, not to control. Let my leadership create a culture of respect, justice, and compassion. Give me the wisdom I need for every decision, big or small.
Help me stay humble, even in success. May my life and leadership always reflect Your love and truth.
In Jesus' name, Amen.

CHAPTER 13

Restoring Relationships — The Role of Healing and Forgiveness in Leadership

"And be kind to one another, tenderhearted, forgiving one another, even as God in Christ forgave you."—Ephesians 4:32 (NKJV)

Leadership isn't just about reaching goals—it's about people. Whether you're leading in business, ministry, school, or your family, relationships are at the center of it all. When people feel hurt, misunderstood, or betrayed, those wounds can create walls that damage trust. Good leaders learn how to bring healing by offering forgiveness and leading with love.

Joseph's story shows us what that kind of leadership looks like. Even after his brothers sold him into slavery, Joseph didn't seek revenge. Instead, when he saw them again years later, he forgave them and helped them during a time of need. That takes great strength and faith. Joseph led with a heart that was healed, not hardened.

Joseph Forgives His Brothers

Joseph had every reason to be angry at his brothers. They betrayed him, sold him into slavery, and walked away from his pain. But when they stood before him years later, Joseph chose a different path—he chose forgiveness.

He said,

> *"I am Joseph your brother, whom you sold into Egypt. But now, do not therefore be grieved or angry with yourselves because you sold me here; for God sent me before you to preserve life. For these two years the famine has been in the land, and there are still five years in which there will be neither plowing nor harvesting. And God sent me before you to preserve a posterity for you in the earth, and to save your lives by a great deliverance. So now it was not you who sent me here, but God." — Genesis 45:4–8 (NKJV)*

Joseph forgave with his words and his actions. He gave his brothers food and a safe place to live. Forgiveness didn't make the past disappear—but it brought peace and unity to his family. This kind of leadership leaves a legacy.

Healing and Forgiveness Go Together

Healing your heart and forgiving others go hand in hand. Forgiveness helps your soul recover from hurt and frees you to lead with a clean heart. Without it, wounds turn into bitterness, and walls go up between you and others. God desires leaders to be whole—inside and out.

> *"Beloved, I pray that in every way you may succeed and prosper and be in good health [physically], just as [I know] your soul prospers [spiritually]." — 3 John 2 (AMP)*

Joseph forgave his brothers before they ever said sorry. God had already done deep healing work in his heart while he was in prison. Forgiveness isn't just for the other person—it's for your freedom too. It's how God prepares you to lead well.

Why Leaders Need to Forgive

When leaders don't deal with their pain, it can shape how they treat others. They might become guarded, overly strict, or even harsh. That's why the Bible tells us to let go of bitterness and trust God to make things right.

> *"Beloved, do not avenge yourselves, but rather give place to wrath; for it is written, 'Vengeance is Mine, I will repay,' says the Lord."* — Romans 12:19 (NKJV)

Unforgiveness doesn't stay hidden. It spreads and affects the way we lead and relate to others. If we don't forgive, it can lead to:

- A fear of trusting others
- Misunderstanding people's motives
- Emotional stress and bottled-up anger
- Walls that block real connection and teamwork

Forgiveness, on the other hand, brings peace. It allows us to move forward instead of staying stuck in the past. Joseph forgave long before his brothers came to Egypt. That's why he was able to respond with compassion and grace when they needed help.

Forgiveness Creates a Healthy Culture

Forgiveness doesn't stay private—it shapes the whole team. When a leader forgives, it teaches others to do the same. It builds a culture of grace, honesty, and second chances. Unforgiveness, on the other hand, creates fear and silence.

> *"Let all bitterness, wrath, anger, clamor, and evil speaking be put away from you, with all malice. And be kind to one another, tenderhearted, forgiving one another, even as God in Christ forgave you." — Ephesians 4:31–32 (NKJV)*

Joseph's forgiveness brought healing not just to him but to his whole family. He turned a painful past into a powerful future. Leaders can do the same by choosing grace and leading with love. That's how transformation begins.

When leaders choose forgiveness, they:

- Create safety for others to grow
- Encourage honesty and teamwork
- Heal past hurts and move forward

Choosing forgiveness as a leader builds a place where people can trust, learn, and try again. When people aren't afraid of being punished for mistakes, they're more willing to grow. This kind of grace builds strong teams. It also reflects the heart of God.

Leading with Honor, Grace, and Trust

To build a strong team, leaders must honor people, give grace, and earn trust. Honor means seeing others the way God sees them—not by their failures but by their value. Grace gives room for people to fall and get back up. Trust is built by being honest, consistent, and caring in every interaction.

> *"Bearing with one another, and forgiving one another, if anyone has a complaint against another; even as Christ forgave you, so you also must do."* — Colossians 3:13 (NKJV)

Joseph lived this out in his leadership. He didn't pretend the betrayal never happened—but he didn't let it define his actions. Instead, he forgave, protected, and provided for the same brothers who hurt him. That kind of leadership builds something that lasts.

Honor, grace, and trust are like bricks in a strong foundation. They hold people together through tough times. When leaders model these values, others follow. That's how lasting culture is built.

Rebuilding Broken Trust

Sometimes leaders break trust—or others break it with them. But even broken trust can be rebuilt with time, truth, and humility. The key is to be honest about the pain and committed to healing. Joseph shows us how powerful restored trust can be.

> *"Repay no one evil for evil. Have regard for good things in the sight of all men. If it is possible, as much as depends on you, live peaceably with all men."* — Romans 12:17–18 (NKJV)

Joseph didn't ignore what happened. He acknowledged the wrong, chose to forgive, and took steps to rebuild. He showed that trust can be restored when grace and wisdom work together. Rebuilding isn't fast—but it is possible.

Joseph shows us how:

- **Acknowledge the hurt**: Don't pretend it didn't happen.

- **Show consistency**: Be honest and steady over time.

- **Set healthy boundaries**: Rebuild trust with wisdom.

- **Give grace**: Allow room for others to change.

When leaders choose to do these things, they build stronger teams. They also teach others how to grow through hard things. Restored trust brings peace. It also opens new doors for leadership and connection.

Kingdom Leadership Focuses on People

True leadership in God's Kingdom is centered on people—not just results. Jesus led this way, always choosing service over status and compassion over control. He forgave Peter when he failed and restored Thomas when he doubted. That's the kind of love and patience that Kingdom leaders are called to show.

> *"For even the Son of Man did not come to be served, but to serve, and to give His life a ransom for many." — Mark 10:45 (NKJV)*

> *"Blessed are the peacemakers, for they shall be called sons of God." — Matthew 5:9 (NKJV)*

Kingdom leaders are not here to dominate—they're here to restore. They forgive, heal, and build bridges where others see walls. They make peace in tense places and bring people together. When we lead like Jesus and forgive like Joseph, our leadership brings lasting hope.

Reflection Questions

1. Are there any broken relationships that may be affecting your

leadership or peace?

2. What's one step you can take to forgive someone who has hurt or disappointed you?

3. How can you lead with more grace, kindness, and a heart open to healing?

Faith Steps

- **Pray for Wisdom to Forgive:** Ask God to show you any relationships that need healing. Pray for the courage and humility to take the first step.

- **Reach Out in Grace:** Choose one strained relationship and commit to having a kind, honest conversation that invites peace and understanding.

- **Model Forgiveness:** Look for ways to show grace in your leadership—especially in difficult situations. Let others see the power of forgiveness in action.

Scripture Meditation

"And be kind to one another, tenderhearted, forgiving one another, even as God in Christ forgave you." — Ephesians 4:32 (NKJV)

Meditation Reflection

Joseph had every reason to stay bitter. His brothers betrayed him. He was sold into slavery and later thrown in prison for something he didn't do. But when the chance came to get even, Joseph chose something better—he forgave.

Years later, when Joseph saw his brothers again, he didn't act out of anger. He showed mercy. Joseph realized that God had used even the pain in his life for a bigger purpose—to save lives and fulfill His plan.

Forgiveness is hard, especially when the wounds are deep. But unforgiveness doesn't just hold others back—it holds us back too. It clouds our thinking, limits our leadership, and keeps us from walking fully in God's purpose.

Ephesians 4:32 reminds us that forgiveness is part of the Christian life. Just as Jesus forgave us, we're called to forgive others. Forgiveness doesn't always mean restoring every relationship, but it does mean releasing the hurt and trusting God to handle the rest.

When you lead with forgiveness, you open the door to healing—not just for others, but for yourself. You create a work or home environment where people feel safe, valued, and seen. Like Joseph, your decision to forgive can lead to restoration, unity, and impact far beyond what you imagine.

Key Meditation Points

- **Forgiveness Heals the Heart:** Letting go of bitterness brings freedom and peace—for you and those around you.

- **Forgiveness Reflects God's Love:** When you forgive, you show the same grace that God gives you. It's a powerful example of Christ's heart.

- **Forgiveness Builds Trust:** Leading with compassion and mercy creates a culture of respect and healing in your leadership.

Prayer for Forgiveness and Healing

Dear God,
Thank You for Joseph's story and the powerful reminder that forgiveness leads to healing. Help me to let go of any hurt or bitterness in my heart. Show me where I need to forgive and give me the strength to do it, even when it's hard.
I ask You to bring healing to broken relationships and peace to places of tension. Help me lead with kindness and create a culture of grace and honor. Thank You for forgiving me, and help me do the same for others.
In Jesus' name, Amen.

CHAPTER 14

KINGDOM INFLUENCE—WALKING IN AUTHORITY WITH HUMILITY

"Then God said, 'Let Us make man in Our image, according to Our likeness; let them have dominion over the fish of the sea, over the birds of the air, and over the cattle, over all the earth and over every creeping thing that creeps on the earth.'" —Genesis 1:26 (NKJV)

Joseph's life teaches us what true influence looks like. He didn't chase power or attention. Instead, he walked in integrity, served faithfully, and trusted God through every season. Because of that, God raised him up to lead during one of the most important moments in history.

When famine hit the land, Joseph didn't panic or try to save only himself. He used his wisdom and authority to help others, including people from different nations. That's Kingdom influence—when your leadership brings life, order, and peace to those around you. Joseph's story shows us that real leadership isn't about control; it's about service.

What Is Kingdom Dominion?

Dominion means using your God-given authority to bless others, not to boss them around. It's about showing love, offering solutions, and living out God's truth in everyday places—like your school, job, or home. In Genesis 47, Joseph used his position in Egypt to organize food storage and prevent a nation from starving. He didn't use power selfishly—he managed it with care and wisdom.

When people came to him in need, he helped them survive and rebuild their lives. He created systems that were fair and smart, showing that dominion includes planning and responsibility. God gives influence so we can lead with excellence and compassion. That's what Joseph did, and it's what we're called to do too.

Authority Comes from God

True authority isn't something we grab—it's something God gives. In Matthew 28:18, Jesus said that all authority in heaven and on earth belongs to Him. He then gave His followers that same authority to represent Him on earth. Joseph understood this and always gave God the credit for his success.

> *"But you shall receive power when the Holy Spirit has come upon you; and you shall be witnesses to Me in Jerusalem, and in all Judea and Samaria, and to the end of the earth."* — Acts 1:8 (NKJV)

This kind of spiritual authority isn't earned by status or money. It comes through obedience, prayer, and walking closely with God. Joseph carried this authority because he honored God in every season of his life.

Leading with Wisdom and Humility

Joseph was a wise and humble leader, and both qualities worked together. The Bible tells us in Proverbs 4:7, *"Wisdom is the principal thing; therefore get wisdom. And in all your getting, get understanding."* Wisdom is knowing how to make good decisions with God's help. Joseph's decisions protected thousands of people because he didn't rely on himself—he leaned on God.

Even when Pharaoh asked him to interpret a dream, Joseph replied with humility: *"It is not in me; God will give Pharaoh an answer of peace."* (Genesis 41:16 NKJV). That's what real humility looks like—knowing you need God every step of the way. God can trust humble people with great influence.

Growing in Your Calling

God didn't put Joseph in charge of Egypt right away—he had to grow first. He learned responsibility by managing Potiphar's house and then overseeing the prison. Each step prepared him for the next. That's why Proverbs 22:29 says, *"Do you see a man who excels in his work? He will stand before kings; he will not stand before unknown men."*

No matter what job you have now, give it your best. God sees everything and uses every assignment to shape your future. Even small tasks matter when you do them with purpose. Excellence opens doors you don't even see yet.

Using Your Influence for Good

When God gives you influence, it's not just for your benefit—it's so you can lift others up. Joseph used his position to help his family, even though they had betrayed him. Instead of revenge, he chose restoration. That's what it means to lead with a Kingdom heart.

The Bible encourages us to stay rooted in godly character, where mercy and truth are not just values but a lifestyle. *Let not mercy and truth forsake you; bind them around your neck, write them on the tablet of your heart, and so find favor and high esteem in the sight of God and man." —Proverbs 3:3–4 (NKJV).* When you lead with kindness and honesty, others begin to trust your voice. As your character deepens, so does your influence.

Boldness with a Godly Strategy

Joseph was bold, but he wasn't reckless. He listened to God, made plans, and acted with confidence when the time was right. In moments of uncertainty, he chose courage over fear.

> *"Have I not commanded you? Be strong and of good courage; do not be afraid, nor be dismayed, for the Lord your God is with you wherever you go." — Joshua 1:9 (NKJV)*

Leaders who walk with God don't rush into decisions. They pray first, wait for instruction, and follow divine strategies. That's how Joseph led—and that's how we should too.

Reflection Questions

1. Where has God placed you to lead or influence others right now?

2. What skills or areas of wisdom do you need to grow in to become a stronger leader?

3. How can you lead with boldness and purpose while staying humble and trusting God's timing?

Faith Steps

- **Pray for Clarity:** Ask God to show you the areas where He has given you influence—at home, work, church, or in your community.

- **Strengthen One Skill:** Pick one practical area to grow in this week—whether it's communication, planning, or leadership development—and take one step to improve.

- **Take a Bold Step:** Do one courageous thing this week that aligns with God's purpose for your leadership, such as starting a project, mentoring someone, or speaking up for truth.

Scripture Meditation

"Then God blessed them, and God said to them, 'Be fruitful and multiply; fill the earth and subdue it; have dominion over the fish of the sea, over the birds of the air, and over every living thing that moves on the earth.'" — Genesis 1:28 (NKJV)

Meditation Reflection

From the beginning, God gave us the responsibility to lead and care for what He created. This calling isn't just about authority—it's about stewardship. It means using our influence to build up others, shape culture with truth, and lead with love and integrity.
Joseph lived this out beautifully. Even when he was mistreated, he remained faithful. When the time came, he didn't use his position in Egypt to serve himself—he used it to save lives and bring healing. His leadership wasn't about control—it was about caring for people and fulfilling God's plan.
Walking in dominion today means doing the same. Whether you lead a team, a classroom, a business, or your household, you're called to lead with wisdom and compassion. God's version of leadership looks like humility, service, and bold action rooted in His truth.

Don't wait until you feel "ready." Start by being faithful where you are. Let God guide your steps, and trust that He is preparing you to influence others in a way that honors Him.

Key Meditation Points

- **You're Called to Influence:** God's command to have dominion means leading with purpose and bringing His values into the places you serve.

- **True Authority Is Stewardship:** Like Joseph, lead with responsibility, not control—serving others and managing well what God has given you.

- **Humility Leads to Promotion:** When you stay humble and trust God, He will open the right doors at the right time.

Prayer for Kingdom Leadership

Dear God,
Thank You for trusting me with influence. Help me to lead with humility, courage, and wisdom. Teach me to use what You've given me to bless others and bring Your truth wherever I go.
Give me the boldness to step into new opportunities and the grace to stay humble in every season. Help me grow in skill, compassion, and purpose so that my leadership honors You.
I commit my plans, ideas, and influence to You. Guide my steps and help me create spaces where people feel valued, truth is upheld, and Your Kingdom is made known.
In Jesus' name, Amen.

CHAPTER 15

Lead with Purpose—Strategy and Stewardship in the Marketplace

"And whatever you do, do it heartily, as to the Lord and not to men, knowing that from the Lord you will receive the reward of the inheritance; for you serve the Lord Christ." —Colossians 3:23–24 (NKJV)

God is raising up leaders who carry His heart into places beyond the church. These leaders work in hospitals, schools, city halls, and offices. Their assignments may not look "spiritual," but their impact is Kingdom. When you lead with God's purpose in the marketplace, your work becomes worship and your influence becomes ministry.

Marketplace leadership is more than doing a job—it's about doing God's work in everyday spaces. Whether you're a teacher, a manager, a student, or an entrepreneur, God has placed you where you are for a reason. Through wisdom, service, and faithfulness, you show others what His Kingdom looks like in real life. That's what Joseph did in Egypt, and that's what God invites us to do today.

Joseph Was a Marketplace Leader

Joseph never held a microphone or stood on a stage—he led in government. His job was to manage food, people, and resources during a time of crisis. Yet he still honored God in every task. Joseph didn't just save Egypt—he influenced nations with strategy, mercy, and faith.

Joseph kept his eyes on God's promises, even when success came. *"And Joseph said to his brethren, 'I am dying; but God will surely visit you, and bring you out of this land to the land of which He swore to Abraham, to Isaac, and to Jacob.'"* (Genesis 50:24, NKJV) Joseph led with vision and never let his power pull him away from his faith. His example reminds us that we can lead with purpose and stay rooted in God's promises.

Strategy Is Part of God's Plan

God gives us more than dreams—He gives us the wisdom to build them. Joseph was given insight to store grain during Egypt's seven good years so people wouldn't starve during the seven bad ones. That strategy saved lives, proved Joseph's faithfulness, and showed that planning is a spiritual gift. Strategy is part of leadership when it comes from God.

When we don't know what to do, we can ask for His wisdom. *"If any of you lacks wisdom, let him ask of God, who gives to all liberally and without reproach, and it will be given to him."* (James 1:5, NKJV) God cares about our daily choices and long-term goals. He wants to lead us in our business, schoolwork, and decisions with clarity and peace.

Stewardship Means Taking Care of What God Gives You

Stewardship means managing what God gives you with care and honor. Joseph didn't waste time, money, or resources—he used everything for

God's glory. He protected the people during famine and used his power to serve, not to take. That's what faithful stewardship looks like.

Joseph reminds us to take every job seriously, no matter how big or small. *"Whatever you do, do it heartily, as to the Lord and not to men."* (Colossians 3:23, NKJV) God sees our efforts and blesses our obedience. Good stewardship builds trust with people and with God.

Mentoring Others Is Part of Leadership

Joseph wasn't just a problem solver—he was a mentor. He gave Pharaoh advice, led entire teams, and helped others grow in their roles. That's what real leadership looks like: lifting others up while you serve. Mentoring multiplies your impact and extends your influence.

Paul gives this instruction: *"And the things that you have heard from me among many witnesses, commit these to faithful men who will be able to teach others also."* (2 Timothy 2:2, NKJV) You don't have to know everything to be a mentor—you just need to be willing to share what God has taught you. When we help others grow, we help the Kingdom grow.

Your Legacy Is What You Leave Behind

Joseph didn't live forever, but his impact did. His leadership, faith, and service blessed generations to come. Legacy isn't about titles or money—it's about the lives you touch and the example you leave. A life of love, wisdom, and faith is the greatest legacy of all.

"A good man leaves an inheritance to his children's children, but the wealth of the sinner is stored up for the righteous." (Proverbs 13:22, NKJV) What you do today matters for the people who come after you. Your kindness, your courage, and your obedience will ripple through time. You are writing a story that others will remember.

The Marketplace Is Your Mission Field

You don't need a pulpit to do God's work—you just need to be faithful where you are. Whether you're working in a hospital, sweeping floors, or leading a business, your work matters. God uses ordinary places to do extraordinary things. The marketplace is your mission field.

> "A good man deals graciously and lends; he will guide his affairs with discretion. Surely he will never be shaken; the righteous will be in everlasting remembrance." — Psalm 112:5–6 (NKJV)

When you lead with love, wisdom, and integrity, people see God in you. And when that happens, your workplace becomes a place of Kingdom influence. Joseph didn't need to be a priest to serve God—he simply walked in obedience and let God do the rest. His story teaches us that every role, every job, and every moment can be holy when it's surrendered to God.

As you finish this journey through Joseph's life, remember this: you are a marketplace leader. You are chosen, equipped, and sent to be a light wherever God has placed you. So lead boldly. Love deeply. Serve faithfully. And build the Kingdom—one decision, one relationship, one act of obedience at a time.

This is your call. This is your moment. You were made for this.

A Personal Prayer: Stepping into My Joseph Calling

Heavenly Father,
Thank You for choosing me to be a modern-day Joseph. I believe You have called me to lead, influence, and bring change wherever You've placed me—in my community, my work, and the world around me. I receive that calling with a humble and open heart.

Just like You gave Joseph wisdom, favor, and strategy, I ask You to give those gifts to me as well.

Let Your favor go before me. Open doors that no one else can open. Help me to walk in honesty and live with integrity. As Psalm 5:12 says, "For You, O Lord, will bless the righteous; with favor You will surround him as with a shield." Surround me with Your protection and guide my every step.

Lord, I need Your wisdom in my decisions. Just like Joseph received understanding to help lead a nation, I ask You to give me insight, clarity, and bold ideas. Your Word says in James 1:5 that if I ask for wisdom, You will give it freely. Help me to think clearly, act boldly, and always trust Your direction.

When things get hard or take longer than I expected, help me not to give up. Remind me of Galatians 6:9: "Let us not grow weary while doing good, for in due season we shall reap if we do not lose heart." Give me the strength to keep going, even when I can't see the full picture.

Anoint my hands to build, my mind to plan, and my heart to lead with love and compassion. Use my influence to bring healing, justice, and hope to the people and places You've called me to serve. Help me to stay humble, knowing that real success comes from following Your will—not chasing fame or approval.

Bless my family, my work, my finances, and my relationships. Help me leave behind a legacy of faith, wisdom, and Kingdom impact. Let everything I do point others back to You.

I believe I am chosen, prepared, and ready for this moment.
Thank You for trusting me with this, Joseph calling.
Let my life show Your goodness, Your grace, and Your power.
In Jesus' name, Amen.

ACKNOWLEDGEMENTS

First and foremost, we give all glory and honor to God—the Author and Finisher of our faith. These Joseph books are not just a collection of principles and stories; they are prophetic blueprints born in the secret place, shaped through obedience, and sealed by grace. Every page reflects His wisdom, His presence, and His Kingdom purpose.

To our families—thank you for your unwavering love and sacrificial support. To our beloved spouses, Pam and Michael, your steadfast commitment and prayer covering have been pillars of strength throughout this journey. To our children, your encouragement, grace, and quiet inspiration remind us of the next generation we are building for.

To one another—as co-authors, co-laborers, and co-founders of the Global Joseph Initiative, thank you for walking this journey in step with the Spirit and in unity of vision. It is an honor to serve together in raising up modern-day Josephs—leaders of influence, integrity, and prophetic authority—across every sphere of society.

To our spiritual mentors, prayer warriors, and apostolic voices—you helped birth this work in the Spirit. Your wisdom, intercession, and timely words of encouragement have strengthened us in ways words cannot express.

To our creative and technical team—editors, designers, formatters, and publishing partners—thank you for your excellence. Our behind-the-scenes work helped transform vision into reality, and your attention to detail has made this series both beautiful and accessible.

To our dear friends, readers, ministry partners, and fellow visionaries—thank you for your prayers, support, and belief in this work. You are part of this story, and we are grateful for your companionship on this Kingdom journey.

And to *you*, our readers—whether you are in the pit, the prison, or the palace—know that you were never forgotten by God. May this series equip you to rise with bold faith, wisdom, and divine strategy. May the Spirit of Joseph rest upon you as you lead with integrity, steward with excellence, and transform your sphere of influence.

If this book has impacted you, please consider leaving a review online. Your testimony not only encourages us—it helps others discover the message and find their own path to purpose.

With deepest gratitude and Kingdom love,
Darrell "Coach D" Andrews & Dr. Shannon A. Austin

ABOUT THE AUTHORS

Darrell "Coach D" Andrews

Darrell "Coach D" Andrews is a dynamic minister, bestselling author, and visionary thought leader who brings bold faith, real-world wisdom, and contagious passion to every platform he touches. As a marketplace minister, he equips leaders to activate their God-given purpose—empowering them to lead with conviction, courage, and Kingdom strategy.

With over two decades of global impact, Coach D has served as a transformational force in Fortune 500 companies, educational institutions, government agencies, and faith-based organizations across North America and beyond. His presentations blend motivation, strategy, and spiritual insight, offering a holistic approach to leadership, reinvention, and cultural transformation.

Coach D holds the prestigious CSP (Certified Speaking Professional) designation, a distinction earned by fewer than 600 speakers worldwide. From post-pandemic leadership and self-care systems to Kingdom entrepreneurship and personal reinvention, Coach D releases more than motivation—he births movement.

He is a devoted husband of 30 years and proud father of four, modeling perseverance, humility, and unwavering faith in God. His voice is a prophetic trumpet calling leaders into alignment with Heaven's blueprint for transformation and revival.

Books by Darrell "Coach D" Andrews:

- *The Purpose Living Teen: A Teen's Guide to Living Your Dreams*
- *Believing the HYPE: Seven Keys to Motivating Students of Color*
- *The Parent As Coach: Developing a Family Dream Team*
- *How to Find Your Passion and Make a Living at It*
- *Reinvention: The Pathway to Job Search Success*
- *The Self-Care Movement*
- *Post-Pandemic Leadership: The Key to Recruitment and Retention*
- Featured in *Chicken Soup for the African-American Soul* ("5 Garbage Bags and a Dream")

Through these works, Coach D continues to uplift and equip diverse audiences with strategies that merge Kingdom values and practical application—mobilizing the next generation of purpose-driven leaders to step boldly into their divine assignments.

Dr. Shannon A. Austin, Ph.D., M.S., B.S.

Dr. Shannon A. Austin is a prophetic voice, thought leader, and spirit-empowered intercessor called to advance the Kingdom of God through prayer, leadership, and transformational ministry. Raised in the Catholic tradition and radically transformed by the power of the Holy Spirit, Dr. Austin carries a mantle of healing, deliverance, and strategic activation for leaders, families, and intercessory teams. Her ministry is marked by an unwavering devotion to prayer, deep intimacy with God, and a heart for restoration and identity alignment.

She holds a Ph.D. in Instructional Management and Leadership, an M.S. in Rehabilitation Counseling, and a triple-major B.S. in Business Administration, Organizational Leadership, and Social & Behavioral Science. Her educational background blends research-backed insights with real-world strategies to help individuals build resilience and achieve lasting success.

Shannon Austin has over 20 years of experience in workforce development, vocational rehabilitation, and human resources; she has dedicated her career to empowering others, fostering resilience, and creating innovative communities and workplaces. Her deep commitment to authenticity and empowerment is reflected in her company's core values of compassion, growth, community, and excellence.

She is a devoted wife of 35 years and proud mother of five, fully understanding the challenges of balancing personal and professional life while staying anchored in the Word of God. Her writings and ministry invite readers into a deeper walk with Christ.

Books by Dr. Shannon A. Austin:

- *The Strength Within: Unlocking the Secrets of Resilience*
- *Unlocking Your Potential: Transforming Your Life with the Eight Pillars of Self-Care*
- *The Roadmap to Success: Strategic Life Planning for the 12 Areas of Life*
- *Family Is a Mosaic Picture: A Journey Through Brokenness, Belonging, and Becoming in the Hands of the Master Craftsman*

Dr. Austin writes to inspire readers to trust in God's plan, embrace spiritual maturity, and pursue their God-given purpose with boldness. With a compassionate heart and a steadfast belief that every person has a role in God's redemptive story, she continues to build bridges of healing, hope, and purpose through her books, teachings, and prayer ministry.

Co-Founders of the Global Joseph Initiative

Darrell "Coach D" Andrews and Dr. Shannon A. Austin are the visionary co-founders of the Global Joseph Initiative (globaljosephinitiative.org), a faith-based movement committed to raising up modern-day Josephs—leaders of influence, integrity, and prophetic authority—who transform culture in government, business, education, media, ministry, and beyond.

The Global Joseph Initiative equips faith-driven leaders with prophetic vision, practical tools, and spiritual wisdom to lead during seasons of both famine and abundance. Through devotionals, training, summits, and coaching, this initiative commissions Kingdom leaders to steward resources, unlock innovation, and lead cultural reformation through the Spirit of Joseph.

To learn more, partner with the movement, or invite Darrell or Shannon to speak, visit www.globaljosephinitiative.org or email **info@globaljoseph initiative.org**.

Co-Authored Series

Marketplace Leadership Series

- *Joseph and Marketplace Ministry: Leadership, Entrepreneurship, and Kingdom Impact*

- *Joseph's Mantle and Marketplace Ministry: A 30-Day Devotional for Kingdom Leaders*

Joseph Leadership for Emerging Voices

- *Joseph & Marketplace Ministry: A Simple Guide to Kingdom Leadership*
- *Joseph & Marketplace Ministry Devotional: A 30-Day Guide to Living Your Calling*

www.ingramcontent.com/pod-product-compliance
Lightning Source LLC
Chambersburg PA
CBHW070508100426
42743CB00010B/1788